The Open Secret of Polyglots

How to Learn English

or Other Languages with Kindle, Print or Audio Books

by

Mihaly Hevesi

M&H Publishing Sz/V

FOR ORDERING INFORMATION OR SPECIAL DISCOUNTS FOR BULK PURCHASES PLEASE CONTACT:

hevesim@yahoo.com

Edited by Jeremy Parrott

Cover design by linguaW

www.linguaw.com

ISBN: 978-963-08-6629-3

to Marcell and Éva

TABLE OF CONTENTS

Acknowledgments

There is not enough room to thank everyone who helped and encouraged me along the way, so I will just mention four: Mario Rinvolucri, Jeremy Parrott, Marcell Hevesi and Emese Szarka.

Thanks to Mario Rinvolucri who has always inspired me to teach imaginatively and who introduced Bernard Dufeu's fantastic language teaching system to me, the PLA (also described in this book). Bernard'system opened new perspectives to me.

The English version of this book would not have been possible without the advice and very active support from Jeremy Parrott who also edited and corrected the manuscript.

My son Marcell Hevesi contributed to this book and method by his natural steps in language acquisition. Watching him grow into his own native language, Hungarian, and now into different foreign languages (German, English) I realized the importance of rhythm and melody that are essential in the process, maybe more important even than pronunciation or memorising words and phrases.

But my utmost thanks go to the active teachers and perseverant language learners like Emese Szarka. She is a very active reader of my books and applies the techniques described here both in her language teaching and learning.

Chapter I

Introduction

A few month ago I purchased a Kindle e-book reader and tried out my language learning techniques using it. The technique goes back partly to the experience learned by famous polyglots (people speaking many languages at a very high level) such as Kató Lomb, Giuseppe Mezzofanti and Heinrich Schliemann, and was partly designed by me for my personal needs and those of my language students. I call the technique Autorhythmy.

In this book you'll learn how to use this technique both with a print book and an e-book reader.

You'll also learn how to listen to audio texts in a foreign language.

This book is meant to be practical. But I'd also like to sensitize you to certain attitudes towards language learning which are probably more important than techniques alone. These attitudes help you to achieve your goal of language acquisition and to stick with the process over the longer term.

Each of the above-mentioned personalities in their time succeeded in learning at least a dozen languages. Kató Lomb used 16 as an interpreter and translator (all in all she learnt 26), Heinrich Schliemann learnt 20, and the legendary Mezzofanti was said to speak 102 languages.

Actually one of the common techniques of these polyglots, who lived in different ages, was reading books in foreign languages.

We can learn a lot from their experiences and techniques. But we can learn from them important attitudes towards language learning as well. You can learn about their lives in Chapter IX in this book.

Although I will use some basic terms concerning the use of e-book readers for Autorhythmy, this book won't give detailed technical specifications about them as they may vary from one model to another. You'll find those details in the manual to your own gadget.

This book is divided into nine Chapters. In the opening three you'll learn about the beginnings of this method (Kató Lomb's language learning system), about attitudes towards language learning and conditions for successful language learning.

In Chapter IV you will learn the basic technique of Autorhythmy, which means learning how to read a book in a foreign language 'without a dictionary'. Here you'll find also how to use this technique with Kindle or other e-book readers. After this you'll read about keeping a reader's diary and making notes on the newly read texts. How to review your notes is explained in Chapter VI.

In Chapter VII you will learn how to listen to audio texts in order to improve your understanding of the spoken language. In that chapter you'll also learn about exercises that can prepare best you for speaking a foreign language. Then a strategic plan for language learning and parallel reading will be described. In Chapter VIII you'll learn how to read a practical book in your native language to get the most out of it. You may use the suggestions there even for a foreign language you have a good command of. Furthermore you will find suggestions in this chapter about how to learn the letters of non-Latin scripts.

Finally in Chapter IX you will read about famous polyglots, interesting methods and theories which were influential in developing the ideas presented in this book.

This Book is Meant for You...

- •if you are a beginner or an advanced learner of English or other languages. You may learn to use reading and listening in a foreign language in order to collect a vast vocabulary from a foreign language in an entertaining way. I'll touch not only upon understanding the written texts, but also on how to understand audio text or speech. Those exercises will help you to improve your listening skills, too;

- •if you already read books in English or other foreign languages, you can learn to use a method that helps you to do it more efficiently. The basics and the suggested exercises (among others Making Notes or Reader's diary) will help you to do this;

- •if you would like to learn more foreign languages and at the same time to learn a basic method that helps you achieve this. The reading technique presented here is based on techniques of renowned polyglots who learnt dozens of languages;

- •if you are a pupil at a high school or a language student at a college and would like to expand your knowledge of the foreign language that you need for your later career;

•if you are a language teacher and would like to broaden your vision of language learning and acquisition, and you want to learn efficient techniques to use with your classes. The majority of the exercises here can be used with pupils or students. Pupils need models. The polyglots presented in this book are in their own way excellent. You could present them to your pupils or students;

•and last but not least if you are a grandma or a grandpa whose grandchildren are living in a foreign country and you would like to learn their new language. Interestingly, many persons enrolling into my courses of Autorhythmy are those very grandmas and grandpas, countering the myth that elderly persons are not able to learn new things, let alone foreign languages. One of the oldest great-grandmas to attend my courses to date was 85. Even now after a few years she still reports in e-mails about books she is reading using this technique.

The Method in a Nutshell

The core of the method - as you will have already realised – is to read a book (usually a novel) in the foreign
language you want to learn.

Reading a book in a foreign language has got many ad-
vantages. It is a very good way of diving into a language.
You can stop reading, jump to previous or subsequent
pages, underline or mark words or phrases, write your
notes in the margin, draw simple pictures etc. In case of
e-books you may highlight words or phrases, add your
notices, search for other places where a certain word
occurs in a different context etc.

Reading a book is the perfect way to encounter frequently occurring linguistic items: vocabulary, phrases,
grammar samples etc. These will come up several times
in a novel while you read it. You get used to them and
internalize them without extra effort as you get into the
text. (Further pros, see later in this book.)

Actually reading books in a foreign language is being
practiced at most universities and colleges by language
students and even at some middle or grammar schools as
well. But there is a big difference between how they usually read and what I'm suggesting here. My suggestion
and that of polyglots is: first read without using a dictionary!

Without a Dictionary!?

Reading a book in the foreign language without using a dictionary? Are you sceptical? Don't be! This is one of the keys that opens up the door to the castle of languages. But how can you read a foreign-language novel without a dictionary if you only understand a few words?

Well, the easiest way to find out the meaning of a new word is to look it up in the dictionary. You only need to open your dictionary or switch to it on one of your gadgets. But does this really lead to the best results? Sometimes you need to know the meaning of a word for immediate use, but sometimes you would like to retain it for a longer time in order to reuse it or to recognize it in a text. In the latter case you can't afford to forget it. But remember the motto: "Easy come, easy go!"

If you don't look it up in the dictionary immediately but rather try to find out its meaning from the context, you'll be investing mental energy. You may have a closer look at the context or be reminded of similar words to the given unknown word in the passage.

If you look up an unknown word in a dictionary right after having read it, you don't invest any mental energy, only physical energy by opening it (not even that if using a digital dictionary). And except for a few words you will forget most of them straight away afterwards.

I hope you agree: you will retain best what you have figured out yourself! And although at first sight it seems more difficult to read a text in a foreign language without looking up each word in a dictionary, it is much more effective and can be much more fun.

If you read a novel or book that really interests you, your curiosity about the details will help you to stay in the text, even if you don't understand the whole thing!

It could seem strange and tiring to read a foreign text without a dictionary. But after the first try you'll understand a lot. Maybe not everything but you'll understand the text globally.

A Secret System?

Actually, there is no secret system for language learning. This book is about reading books (print books, or e-books) and listening to audio texts in foreign languages and not about a secret system. Language schools employing some specific system proclaim their system as the ultimate one. Be sure there is no such a system. For success in language learning you need to use a variety of tools – see page 28: *Success and its Basic Conditions.*

The effectiveness of reading a book in a foreign language without a dictionary is only secret insofar as it is not widespread yet and many people think it is impossible to do or give up too soon, after the first attempt.

Why do We like Reading?

I suppose you like reading. Otherwise you wouldn't have started reading this book. But have you ever put the question to yourself - why do you like reading?

You may come to different answers than the following but I think it is important to think a bit about it. It confirms our confidence in the importance of reading and can make us even more regular readers.

I think reading works because it helps us get into a different state of mind. You may enter a different world compared to your sometimes chaotic everyday life. It allows you to be alone but contented, shutting off disturbances from the outside world.

By reading you may also experience your inner pictures. These pictures may remain partly unconscious or they may come about in an active way as well.

The pictures you see in a movie or television, though sometimes unbeatable, are ready-made. They may be beautiful and full of action but they are someone else's and therefore experiencing them is more passive than letting your own pictures emerge and exploring your own emotions while reading a good book! To put it simply, by reading you enrich your life in an active way!

You experience your uniqueness through these inner pictures (or feelings). For your inner pictures mostly are unique. They are just as much your own as your personal memories. No-one shares them in the same way as you! Yes, your fantasies and inner pictures belong to you.

Interestingly, according to C. G. Jung these pictures are common to all humanity. They can appear while dreaming or daydreaming, in which case you get to a deeper level in your imagination, which has a psychically healing effect.

Inner pictures will have a certain importance even in the technique I'm going present to you in this book.

I have been reading regularly since I developed the taste for reading as a child. I don't want to miss reading. So I read something every day, be it in my native language or in a language that I am practicing or learning at that moment!

My enthusiasm for reading makes learning languages much easier and more interesting than simply learning from course books or on organized courses.

But there are other pros of reading as well - you can tell yours now. Why do you like reading?

All in all the benefits of reading in my view are:

- you enter "a new world";

- you experience your inner pictures;

- you not only train your brain and allow it to build new neuronal structures, but get involved emotionally in the text;

- you learn new experiences from others that you may use for yourself;

Introduction for Language Learners: Learning on your own - Autonomy

Well, reading a good book in a foreign language means learning on your own. You may have laid the foundation of a foreign language at school or by working on your own and you want to get more out of it: grow your vocabulary, talk to native speakers, understand films and lyrics.

But it may also be that you experienced bad language education at school. You may have memorized vocabulary or grammar rule lists that you weren't really able to use and soon forgot again. Now you would like to try something else, something that works.

Yes, it is absolutely essential to get to the point, and be determined that you want to learn a foreign language on your own. Of course you may ask for help from a teacher or native speakers, or use course-books but it's you who'll determine the means and the topics of your language learning programme. No-one knows better about your own interests and preferences than you.

Reading is the best technique for that and for gaining a wide vocabulary. You need vocabulary both for speaking and understanding a language. And you can collect it on your own based on your personal needs.

Introduction for Teachers

Another important reason I have written this book is that, beside language learners, I'd like to encourage language teachers as well. Don't hesitate to tell about this technique or outstanding polyglots and classical language learners mentioned in this book to your pupils or students. Pupils need models who prompt them and demonstrate that, though language learning seems to be a complex affair, it can be accomplished very effectively. If you are a language teacher you'll profit a lot from this, your pupils could be more motivated when hearing about polyglots and their achievements! You'll find short biographies and techniques of some classical polyglots in this book. But you can easily do more research about them in a good library or on the internet! You may even find examples of contemporary polyglots. Don't delay, do it right now!

Another tip for language teachers: you might think of inviting people who speak several languages to your lessons, you're sure to find some in your area. It is bound to be very motivating and inspiring for your students!

As a foreign language teacher I am aware of the fact that, if I don't convince my students to do something in addition to the lessons, they won't get to a fluent level in any foreign language I am teaching them. So I can show them in the lessons how to do various things, how to read books, or how to watch films and how to make notes in order to get the most out of these activities.

Autorhythmy, or the Auto-method

The reading (and listening) techniques that I'm going to present in this book are part of the method I call Autorhythmy. Some people call it simply the auto-method. It was designed for my personal needs and for those of my language students who needed and need to understand conversations, audio texts, films and lyrics; furthermore to speak the foreign language correctly and spontaneously when communicating with native and non-native speakers.

Despite the fact that the exercises in autorhythmy are based on previous techniques of polyglots and some language teaching systems, it is a coherent system that has its own nuances and goals.

Autorhythmy is a mosaic word in which 'auto' stands first of all for autonomy. You need autonomy in language learning. You will determine your language learning programme, and don't necessarily require a teacher or course book, because you know why you want to learn a language, and what your interest areas are! If you get the taste for it, you will enjoy your autonomy in language learning and will find it most effective. Autonomy also means, in my view, that you have got to the point that only you are responsible for your success in language learning.

'Auto' besides the above also refers to my respect and honour for Kató Lomb. She told in a joking way in one of her lectures, that she doesn't own a car (an 'auto'), but she travels in three, at least in the field of language learning!

One of these is 'autolexia' (derived from the Greek: auto – for myself ; lexus- reading), which means - reading for myself , especially books I am really interested in.

The second is, 'autographia' (graphia- write) - write to myself. She kept diaries in different languages.

And the third one is 'autologia' (logos- word, to speak), speak to myself! She also called it autologue instead of monologue. Kató Lomb prepared for interpreting at a conference by speaking the language to herself she had to translate. She could do the autologia – speaking to herself so intensely, that she had forgotten about the environment she was in. She used to say in different lectures that she was once so involved with autologia while preparing for simultaneous translation at a conference in German that while going home in the local bus in Budapest she was surprised by people speaking Hungarian. She asked them with a joyful expression on her face whether they were immigrants or only tourists!

And what does 'rhythmy' stand for?

Well, there are at least two reasons. As a teacher I have tried and worked in different teaching frames. I've been teaching languages to small children at a Waldorf School, where it is important to get the pupils from class 1 onwards acquainted with the rhythm and the melody of the target foreign languages. The rhythm and a melody of a language is very characteristic. You'll recognise a language by its rhythm and melody, even if you don't understand a word of it. Think of Italian, it is unlikely you'll confuse it with any other language, once you have identified it as Italian. (See page 91: *The Waldorf School*.)

If you practice the rhythm and melody of a language you merge into that language. That is actually the basis of how babies get acquainted with their native language as spoken by their parents. In this intensive 'language course' they get the meaning of the phrases and words through sensing the emotions of their parents. The rhythm and melody may play a great role in transmitting these emotions. Yes, babies sense the intention behind language mostly through these elements. Of course there may be other elements, too, to enhance these sensations. One thing is sure though – no-one explains to them the meaning of the words in their infancy. At the beginning that would be quite absurd.

My adventure with Chinese also confirmed the importance of practicing the rhythm and melody of a language. A few years ago, just out of curiosity I started to learn Mandarin. Mandarin or Chinese is a tonal language, which means that one syllable can have different meanings if given a different tonality. For example 'Ma', can mean either 'mother' or 'horse', depending on how you pitch it. If you pitch it on a high even level 'Ma' means mother, whereas in a falling and then rising tone, it means horse. I guess the Chinese have lots of fun, when they hear westerners trying to speak Chinese. Yes, my problem was how to differentiate these tonalities so that I didn't say stupid things.

The answer was actually at hand. I had to get used to them by practicing with the melody and rhythm of the language. Although you don't find such exercises in any course books known to me, there are language acquiring methods where they are practiced. As well as the methods used in Waldorf Schools you can try out Bernard Dufeu's language teaching courses for example – see page 116: *Bernard Dufeu's PLA - Psychodrama for Language Acquisition*). These experiences had an enormous influence on autorhythmy.

Actually practicing the rhythm (clapping your hands, banging on the table etc.) and the melody (humming, buzzing the melody) of a language are important, even if you are learning a non-tonal language. It helps you to get to a better understanding of the spoken language by immersing yourself in it. But it also helps you improve your pronunciation, which needs refreshing from time to time.

'Autorhythmy' also refers to our own rhythm, which is worth considering when practising a foreign language. Our strategy will be based on our own rhythm, spare time and daily routine.

Well, now you know why I have called the method Autorhythmy. But let's have a short review:

Auto stands for autonomy which is important in language learning and in homage to Kató Lomb who told us that she used "auto" techniques;

The rhythm and melody of a language are characteristic, and it is important to practice them in order to get thoroughly familiar with the language.

Chapter II

The Beginnings: About Polyglot Kató Lomb's Technique

As an enthusiastic language learner I was looking for practical ways of language learning when I stumbled upon Kató Lomb's method 25 years ago. Her method was based partly on the techniques of earlier polyglots like Heinrich Schliemann or Giuseppe Mezzofanti, and like many great things it is very simple: just as previously stated, you should take a book, a novel you are interested in and read it in the foreign language without using a dictionary, even at a very early stage of your foreign language acquisition.

At first sight it's very strange and seemingly difficult to read a novel from the very beginning, but I made good progress when I became interested in learning a number of European languages.

I also remember my room-mate at college, to whom I was teaching German and to whom I recommended Kató Lomb's system. It happened when he had been studying German for 3 months or so, that I gave him the German version of *Three Men in a Boat (to say Nothing of the Dog)* by Jerome K. Jerome, which I loved and still love very much. I told my friend to give it a try and to read it without looking up each word in the dictionary. He looked at me perplexed and checked my face, whether I was kidding. However, he started reading it. After a few minutes he just shut the book impatiently and told me that he didn't understand anything except for a very few familiar words.

I gave him only a few tips on how to do it: I told him he should just think about some of the words and phrases and draw his conclusions about the supposed meaning. It would be an intellectual pleasure, and he shouldn't worry, if he was right or not, or didn't understand everything. Then I left him alone. After 15-20 minutes I heard him laugh as a humorous scene was coming somehow through the text to him. I think he didn't understand the whole plot, but this wasn't important in that moment, much more important was that he got the taste of what I had suggested to him, he got the taste of global understanding of a text.

I would like to emphasize this moment as one of the richest in language acquisition. You understand something that seemed foreign to you before. This is a basic experience.

Reading good books is a real joy even in a foreign language and, moreover, this is an incredible way to accumulate a vast and useful vocabulary.

For my part, later on I chose an easier way than that: I reread my favourite books from before in different foreign languages. Understanding is easier when you reread books you liked before. Reviving my favourite moments of a good book gives a very high motivation to go on with language acquisition and not to become tired of it.

In most cases I'll remember what happened in a certain chapter and I'll have a global understanding of the text. I can halt at certain words or phrases and draw a conclusion about the meaning of them. But in many cases you cannot stop because a wave catches you when reading. Kató Lomb says, if a word is important it will occur again and again and you'll retain it.

Kató Lomb rightly noted about her book reading technique that it doesn't prepare you to understand the spoken language and native speakers may have difficulty in understanding the speaker who learns only from reading books or using course books. When reading a text in a newly learnt foreign language the reader reacts automatically with his own or a slightly different articulation. She tried to balance this by engaging in conversations with native speakers and listening to radio programmes as much as possible in the foreign language. Anyway she stated that reading in a foreign language is one technique by which you may gather a comprehensive vocabulary.

These days we can overcome this problem by listening to audiobooks or other audio texts in parallel with reading. If you listen to a text you'll also encounter the rhythmical and melodic characteristics (the prosodic elements) of the language frequently enough to internalize them as well. In autorhythmy we listen to audio texts with appropriate exercises. See page 66: *Listening to Audio Books and Other Texts*!

Success and its Basic Conditions

The polyglots mentioned at the beginning as passionate language learners, besides reading and other important exercises, knew how to approach language learning. That's why they were successful at it and were able to learn a large number of languages. And that is exactly what we need if we want to become successful language learners: the right approach.

You probably don't need as many languages as Kató Lomb was able to work with and you would probably be happy with a few, or even just two. But I guess it's true to say that most of you would agree that: "Besides my native language I'd like to have at least a relatively good command of one foreign language, English, French, Spanish or whatever it may be." You'll need it for your university degree, for your job, for travelling around, for not keeping mum when you have to get into conversation while abroad, or just for reading a good book, to watch a film in another language to enjoy it or to practice the language. The method described here is actually suitable for practising not only English, but any other language you can read the letters of. That means you have reached the first level of reading and gained the basic reading skills in a given foreign language.

Actually my aim in writing books about language learning is to emphasize the fact that anybody who has learnt her or his native language is able to learn 2 or 3 foreign languages.

Times have changed since the above personalities learnt so many languages, even in the short time since Kató Lomb died in 2003 at the age of 93. She used to read books in foreign languages and used the radio to listen to different radio broadcasts. She didn't really experience and use the internet for language learning, let alone i-phones, i-pads or e-book readers. We have the internet and so many technical gadgets now. Practically it seems that there aren't any barriers to learning a foreign language comfortably on our own, or improving our knowledge of a foreign language we have already started. But the question is: Does this really happen?

Successful Language Learning, despite the many technical tools, still remains the privilege of small children being exposed to the language and those who know how to approach language learning and can persevere. Unfortunately we are not taught these approaches at school.

The Basic Conditions for Learning a Language

If you really want to learn a language you need to take responsibility for it. No teacher, course book or special method can guarantee your success. Only you! But don't worry, language learning or acquisition can be joyful and is much more fun then you ever imagined! And if we discover real motivation, it is easy to take responsibility for it (to become a regular learner, search for ways you can accomplish your wish to have a good command of the foreign language).

Let's think a bit about the basic conditions for learning languages. Firstly, you'll need motivation, secondly intensity and perseverance towards learning, and thirdly a healthy attitude towards language learning – and language silence!

Motivation

The pivotal point for success in language learning and acquisition is perseverance! But this will depend on your motivation and attitude.

You may feel the urge to learn a foreign language because you need it for school, your job or your holiday. Is that really motivating? Or you may learn a language because you have fallen in love with it, you like its melody, its rhythm, the mentality of the native speakers etc. Of course the later motivations seem to be much more effective. It is a kind of an inner motivation, while the earlier ones are said to come from outside. But love can be short-lived and your enthusiasm may vanish after the first attempts and challenges.

Therefore if you really want to be motivated you need to find an outer and an inner motivation at the same time. Or to put it in a different way: you have to find an idealistic goal for using the language in the near or distant future. For example, Heinrich Schliemann had a dream he wanted to bring about from his childhood on: he dreamed of finding the mythical Troy he had imagined would prove to be real. To do this he needed languages. And he was proved right. He really found Troy based on Homer's description!

If you have a look at other successful language learners, you'll find an ideal goal there as well. Another polyglot,

Alexander Körösi-Csoma, wanted to find the ancestors of the Hungarians in Asia in the 18th to 19th centuries, so he had to learn languages to be able to travel to India. He learnt about 19 in all. He went to India and unfortunately didn't find any Hungarians there, but he edited the first English-Tibetan dictionary at that time.

I knew someone personally who had learnt Italian, because he wanted to understand something at Dante's Divine Comedy. Something wasn't clear in the translation into his native language and for a certain reason it became very important to him to understand that part, so he started to learn Dante's language.

And what is your motivation? Can you feel that learning languages is somehow linked to your values (preferences) or an ideal goal? If so, you won't face motivation problems!

Another very important piece of advice is the old Latin proverb: Varietas delectat – variety is the spice of life. As Kató Lomb says in one of her 10 suggestions for language learners :

"If your enthusiasm for studying flags too quickly, don't force the issue but don't stop altogether either. Move to some other form of studying, e.g., instead of reading, listen to the radio; instead of writing a composition, poke about in the dictionary."

Intensive Periods of Learning

You'll need to invest time in acquiring a language. Just like a sport, if you want to be good at it, you'll need daily training. In order to learn a language you'll need 12-

14 hours a week for a longer period of time (5-6 months). Actually that is one of the most important rules, at least when you really want to get to a useful level of the language. And paradoxically after such an intensive period of learning you need "language silence", too.

What is "Language Silence"?

To internalize theory (which means being able to use it adequately in practice or to develop skills) you'll need to let your knowledge sleep for a shorter or longer period of time. In language learning I call this language silence.

For me and for many language learners it is an interesting experience when after a period of intensive learning we make a shorter or longer break. When after this break we go on learning, we realize that our skills have progressed on to a higher level: I can speak better, I understand the spoken texts better, my spelling has improved etc. And this is so, even if I felt a bit disappointed before, as I didn't realize how much I had achieved during the learning period. This is like a magic and is very motivating.

What happens during "language silence"? Well, something very important: the units of language we have learnt come together, taking a coherent shape and becoming available for practice.

Maybe the process you went through when you were learning how to drive can make it clear. When you started to practice driving you only knew theoretically how to change gears and push the clutch and let up the gas pedal at the same time (in the case of manual transmission cars). I bet you weren't able do it on the first day, you needed to let your knowledge sleep until you had internalized it.

Only after several days you may have realized that you can do it, and what is more: you can drive in the traffic, you can observe the traffic signs and lights, as well as calculating the necessary braking distance at a given speed.

During language silence (for a few days or weeks) be sure not to do any practice with the language. Then pick up learning again. Sam Betts, a guest teacher in Hungary, had been learning Hungarian very hard for a year when he and his family suddenly had to return to Britain. He was afraid he would forget the language he had invested so much time and energy in. After 10-11 months they returned to Hungary and realized that they were able to use the language at a much higher level than before. His interesting and humorous testimony as told in his story about his adventure with Hungarian, you can read in my book *The Art of learning Languages*(translation in progress).

What if You Don't Have 12-14 Hours a Week for Language Learning?

You have to be realistic. Are you able to fit those 12-14 hours for language learning into your weekly routine? If you cannot, even 15 minutes a day will be helpful for a start. However, it will take much longer to get to a usable knowledge.

In order to accomplish the practice of 12-14 hours a week, - as a working housewife or husband or parent, you should find gaps in your day. Are you traveling by public transport? Maybe then you'll find time to practice the language in one way or another - reviewing your notes, reading a book that interests you, listening to the radio, recordings, music, or even talking to yourself in a foreign language etc. Remember Kató Lomb's auto-exercises!

A Healthy Attitude Towards Language Learning

Your attitude towards language learning is another important point. Well, what do I mean by it? It is not so much about industriousness or "sticking to your plan whatever happens", as about modesty! Kató Lomb said, "You can only be learning a language, but you can never have learnt it." Her long life was highlighted not primarily by a good command of different languages but the actual study of them. Can you identify yourself with this statement? If so, you won't experience it as a defeat when after a learning period you feel you "haven't yet learnt" the language, but will be happy that you have moved forward a bit and are on the road.

Enjoy and Honour Languages

Whatever language you may be learning you can imagine that the language is something very special, very ancient and honourable and at the same time modern, too. This means that, through successive generations, it has helped and helps people to communicate and form a society. You can feel gratitude that you have got the opportunity to learn it, to listen to its sounds, to take its sounds into your mouth, to work with it.

You may also add other thoughts to this.

This kind of "religious" reverence can be felt towards all languages. It is especially helpful for those languages that aren't fashionable to learn or perhaps don't seem so pleasant to the ear.

Gadgets and Books

For learning languages you may use course-books, CD-ROMS, DVDs, i-phones, i-pads, tablets, mini tablets etc. or you may enrol for language courses on different sites. But despite having these options an average language learner may not experience success in language learning. Or after purchasing a tool and after making a very promising start, he or she may lack the motivation to go on. Then the question is: Am I using the right gadgets and tools for learning? Am I using them in the right way?

Well, I am not against technical gadgets, but they did enter our lives rather suddenly. They promise effectiveness but we may realize that they can also cause confusion and an unbalanced psyche into the bargain. Of course if you don't have such experiences skip this sub-chapter, but if you feel the way I do, read on.

This happens because many of these devices offer us so many choices at once that you are tempted to do something else with them instead of learning and enjoying learning.

Have you ever experienced unease while surfing the internet when browsing far away from your original goal?

Actually using a gadget compared to reading a print book is in many aspects very different. A print book is not designed for doing other things than reading. If you are in the right mood it may lead you to your own inner pictures. Our laptop, tablets, i-phones and i-pads, e-book readers may distract us from them. They offer us the mixed pleasures of multi-tasking.

I don't want you to throw away your gadgets - just don't let them distract you. Learn to use them in the right way! And they can enrich your life, but only if you are successful in not letting them distract you from your original goal. For some people this is not a problem, as they have learnt how to concentrate on one thing while studying. In the case of language learning the question is, whether you can stay involved deeply in learning, reading, practicing over a longer time period.

You have to get involved in emotions, to see the inner pictures you imagine while reading. Enjoying a novel or learning a lesson doesn't work if you haven't fully entered into it. That's the way you have to use your gadgets. You have to find a way that allows you to immerse yourself in reading, in emotions for fifteen, thirteen minutes or sometimes for hours without being distracted.

Concentrate on one task you want to accomplish. Multitasking doesn't really work with language learning. It may work in an office or to manage your administrative tasks, but in language learning you won't find it useful!

If you have once determined to sit down and study for half an hour or an hour, don't let get distracted by anything else 'that is important' and can be done 'very quickly' on your gadget!

Determine the task and the time during which you won't do anything else than read, listen to or practise the language. For example: "Now I'm going to read my novel for an hour, and I won't use my gadget for anything else." And stick to it precisely! Don't let even one minute be stolen!

The Kindle E-Book Reader

I have to confess I was rather disillusioned with gadgets, even when I somewhat sceptically bought a new one: a Kindle e-book reader. However, I have now learnt to appreciate and to use it. I use it for what I use a book, to immerse myself in a topic that interests me, or to read in foreign languages.

My Kindle e-book reader has proved to be very useful and really effective tool for reading foreign e-books and practising autorhythmy techniques. It comes with a few dictionaries uploaded that you can use while reading a text. Even though I said that we don't use a dictionary in the beginning of our reading, the dictionary will have an important role to play in the review phase.

The other useful tool on Kindle is a "text to speech" facility which allows you to listen to the text you have on your display. At the moment it is only available for English.

Detailed technical descriptions about how to install new dictionaries, and how to use them while reading you'll find in the instructions to your e-book reader.

A big advantage of Kindle is that, during the phase of investigating a new word, or later on, when reviewing the marked words and phrases, you can search for places where these occur in the book be it on previous or subsequent pages. You can also analyse them there and get closer to the meaning.

Chapter III

Reading in a Foreign Language

If you read a book you really like in English or another language, you'll accumulate a wide vocabulary in an entertaining way. Knowing enough vocabulary items is pivotal in order to use a language.

One of the main rules here is: you should be interested in the text you read. Or in other words: the text should captivate you. That will help you to retain the words and phrases and learn the language without tiresome effort. The more emotions you can attach to it (sadness, happiness etc.), the better your memory will work. If you like romance, read romantic novels; if you like detective stories, read detective stories. That's what Kato Lomb kept saying, and she was absolutely right. In the novels you like, you'll be emotionally involved.

Success will come from your regular practice in reading (or/and listening to audiobooks), and from the appropriate techniques you are using to review your new vocabulary (both will be described soon). If you like reading, you have got one of the best methods in your hands to learn foreign languages!

Beside praising reading its deficiencies have to be mentioned as well. An important shortcoming of reading is - if you are a beginner and even later -, that you'll use your own articulation slightly transformed. That means while reading a text in a foreign language you'll mostly use the pronunciation, the rhythmical and melodic patterns of your native language. Even if you have learnt a bit of pronunciation or orthography of the foreign language. Of course if you have been practicing pronunciation enough this will occur only partially.

We can counterbalance this shortcoming by listening to audiobooks or other audio texts. If you listen to a text you'll also meet the rhythmical and melodic characteristics (the prosodic elements) of the language frequently enough to internalize them as well. In autorhythmy we listen to audio texts using relevant exercises – see page 66: *Listening to audio books and other texts*.

Global Understanding

Global understanding is the point! We don't even understand or hear everything correctly in our native language - we only have a global meaning which was formed by the text, the context, the situation, gestures, and very often by our preconception of the situation.

If you want to get to the global understanding of any kind of written text, don't bother too much about the unknown words, concentrate on the known ones. In fact that is one of the biggest differences between the reading method presented here and reading in a foreign language generally. You'll learn the details at the description of the technique itself.

Kató Lomb says in her book Polyglot: How I learn languages: "It's much more of a problem if the book becomes flavourless in our hands due to the many interruptions, than not learning if the inspector is watching the murderer from behind a blackthorn or a hawthorn."

How to Choose a Book for Reading in a Foreign Language

Well I suppose you have got an idea by now what kind of books you should read in the foreign language you'd like to improve or learn. But let's get through the most important advice concerning this.

Take a book you really want to read and you are interested in. The genres you like in your native language will do just as well in the foreign language (pulp fiction, detective story, romantic story etc.)

Or take a book you had read once in your native language and enjoyed very much. For example as an adolescent I got tremendous pleasure from *The Adventures of Tom Sawyer* and *Huckleberry Finn* by Mark Twain. And later on I enjoyed books by Jerome K. Jerome. I read them again and again in different languages. Just as Heinrich Schliemann read *The Adventures of Telemachus*!

I realize, when I get to my favourite scene or chapter, that the same sensations and atmosphere appear in my mind that I got reading the book in my native language. It is an amazing feeling, that even without understanding the whole vocabulary, I "understand" what happens. In such cases you get into a flow and don't even want to learn the meaning of the unknown words, because you've got the sensation of understanding the text!

If you have the basics of a language, don't use abridged texts or easy text books. Of course if you don't have even the basics you may try using easy texts and abridged novels as well. But remember that easy texts can be flavourless or bloodless. Enjoy the richness of a language, even if you don't understand everything - don't get frustrated by this!

Chapter IV
The Basic Technique

An Experiment before the Technique

Before getting to the finer points of our reading technique I'd suggest a practical experiment. I hope you'll find it interesting and amusing!

The experiment is the following:

Each you make your way to some well-known destination (be it to your school, your work, or to do the shopping…). Describe the way there to yourself silently. Don't do it for more than a minute. But maybe you should close your eyes as well. Please read this book further only after you have done this!

Now answer the following questions:

- Did you see inner pictures while describing the way? Which ones?

- Did you hear noises or voices? Which ones?

- Did you smell scents or odours? Which ones,

- Did you experience the taste of anything? Which ones?

- Did you experience temperature, anything hot, warm, or cold?

Your experiences probably were just as like those who come to the Autorhythmy training. You probably experienced inner pictures as about 95% of the trainees do. About the half of them realize noises or speech as well, and only a few (1-5%) experience even other sensations while reviewing one of their daily routes to a certain destination.

The most important thing to realize from this experiment is that every one of us has got inner pictures while using a language. These pictures may be very personal ones. They mostly originate in our own experiences, and memories, though others may seem unaccountable. But they are somehow connected to our words and phrases. Either the words and phrases summon them up or it happens in the reverse order: the pictures summon up the words and phrases. Well, which came first, the chicken or the egg? This may depend on your personality or state of mind.

Well, the existence of inner pictures and the ability to create them in a conscious way are the bases we can lean on to understand texts globally in a foreign language. Inner pictures that we create about the meaning of the known words in a text will help us to understand also some unknown words and phrases which we meet for the first time in the same text. You'll soon see how it works.

Before getting to the technique itself, please get a book you'd like to read in a foreign language and use it while reading about the technique and do your practice with it. Any book would do that you'd like to read!

The Technique - PERM

You may do a bit of pre-reading of the book, which means that you get the basic information about it by having a look at the cover, table of contents, recommendations, introduction etc. – see page 86: *The First Step - Systematic Skimming.*

Then go through the following points (PERM):

- •PICTURE IT! Start reading the text. Read 2 pages (at least), concentrate only on the words you understand, and make inner pictures of them;

- •EAT the new words (or taste them)! Read the same text again (2 pages) and now concentrate on some of the unknown words.

- •REASON IT OUT! While you are tasting the new words and phrases try to find out their meanings based on the context and words you have understand before. Don't worry if you don't figure them out straight away. Name words you associate with the unknown words;

- •MARK IT! Underline, or in case of e-book readers highlight, the new material - , write your notes, and important phrases/chunks on the margin or in the pop-up window of your e-book reader).

Let's look at it now in detail:

1.PICTURE the Words You understand!

Start reading the text (2 pages at least) and concentrate only on the words you understand. Make inner pictures of them.

Before going into detail about of this point of the technique let me ask you something. How do you usually start to understand a foreign text? How do you or how did you do that at school? I'd be surprised if your answer weren't that you translated it, looking up the unknown words either in a dictionary or in the wordlist at the end of the chapter. So you care or cared about the unknown words or phrases. Well, that is one way you can do it. But if you know the basics of a language you should skip this and do the reverse! First of all don't bother about the unknown words! Yes, leave them alone for the time being! Have a look at those ones that are familiar to you!

Make a start from what you know! Is that different from what you did before? Absolutely! And if you try to do it, you'll find it a bit difficult as you are probably used to going to a dictionary to get the meaning of the unknown words. Fortunately you can get used to this new method very easily and quickly. You may stop for longer at a familiar word in the text to imagine its meaning. Picture it (inner picture)!

Start now, read 2 pages from your chosen book! Then go on reading this book!

Have you finished reading the 2 pages? Could you imagine the meaning of the words that were familiar to you?

In this way you have uncovered some parts of the text. Of course there are still plenty of parts which you don't understand at all. But you have accomplished something very important. You entered a different world, even if it is still vague. You'll work now to make it clearer and clearer. You may now let your fantasy work, you may put the questions: What may happen in the text? What is the text about?

And a real investigation can start now by reading the text for a second time.

When giving feedback in one of my Autorhythmy courses my students called this practice (the first point) "movie watching". They were watching their inner pictures arising while reading. If you are a beginner in the language you won't understand too many words, but even so, you'll have some words you'll find familiar and can make a picture of.

Imagining the words that are familiar to you is a very good exercise when listening to a text, too. It helps you also to improve thoroughly your understanding of the spoken language and audio texts: lyrics, movies, etc. – see page 69: *Improving your understanding of audio texts and real life speech*.

It has to be mentioned that reading by imagining the meaning of the known words can be done throughout a whole book without getting to the next point of our reading technique. Well, it all depends on your goals.

I often read books in languages I haven't been using for a long time in this way, just to immerse myself in the language and to get used to it again. Or simply to repeat the familiar words and phrases of that language. Take care that this doesn't become automatic. When you feel tired of it try to "create" the pictures and add something to it: maybe a new perspective or colour etc.

Understanding- What is it?

Well, according to our concept we could say that understanding in a foreign language is when you have got a clear inner picture of a word/ phrase or context. But that is true only at the beginning and for the practice when you are getting accustomed to it. During this period you care first about the words that are familiar to you. And what happens later on? Should we create inner pictures all the time when reading or listening?

To make this clear let me ask you something: what does it mean that you understand the words and phrases in your native language? Actually you aren't aware of the inner pictures, when talking, listening or reading, are you? In our experiment at the beginning of Chapter IV. you became aware of the pictures, because you answered the questions. And despite this you UNDERSTAND the words/phrases in your native language.

Do you know their definition from a dictionary? I don't think so. It would be quite crazy if we knew that (except for a few, of course!). But even so there is something that signals that you understand a text! And this is nothing else but a feeling! You feel you understand it! So later on after you have reached an advanced level you will also have this feeling when reading or listening in the foreign language. Therefore the answer to the question "Should we create inner pictures all the time when reading or listening?" is: "No, you need it at the beginning, but afterwards you'll have a feeling as to whether you have understood a word or not." Be aware of that feeling!

Skip Decoding

Many language learners try to translate words while speaking or listening. That is very difficult and almost impossible work. We cannot talk to someone or understand anyone fluently by translating his speech word by word. If you've ever tried it you may confirm this. It is a pity that many people experiencing this may give up language learning and conclude that they aren't able to acquire any foreign language. But speaking and talking doesn't mean translating even if course books and vocabulary lists suggest this.

Imagining the familiar words – just as suggested before - will also help to skip unnecessary translation (decoding) and get "right to the meaning" of a word or a text.

By imagining the meaning of the known words being read or spoken we can get to the meaning of them. We can get used to skip translating. Maybe not after the first trials but after 3-4 sessions of practice most people can get to a very high level of doing so. Of course sometimes you will translate some words as well, but more rarely then before, so it won't disturb your fluency in understanding and speaking.

Well, as stated before it depends on your intentions whether you go on with the following points or not. If I want to learn new vocabulary in a conscious way, I continue with the following points.

2.EAT the new words (or taste them)!

Read the same text again and now concentrate on some of the unknown words.

This means that your investigation is starting now! Read the text again and stop at an unknown word or phrase! You don't need to stop at the unknown words. Choose one from each sentence, or even fewer: choose one from two sentences etc. You may choose one, because you think it could be an important word. Choose a maximum of 7-8 unknown words or phrases from the text you read at one sitting by imagining the familiar words. The quantity isn't important but the quality is! Don't worry if there are a lot more unknown words other than those you have analysed. They may recur later on in the text.

From your 2 pages previously read you'll have 7-8 new words you'll be doing the investigation with.

Tasting or eating the word means that you say it and repeat it silently concentrating on the movements of your lips, tongue, jaw etc.! In this way you internalize the word or phrase, so you start to ingest it.

We do this automatically when looking up a word in a dictionary. Watch yourself when trying to find a new word in a print dictionary. You just like me may be murmuring the word, till you find it.

3.REASON it out!

While tasting the new words or phrases analyse their meaning by checking the context you have understood. What may this word or phrase mean?

Give your answers! In many cases you can find out in a very short time or at least have an idea. If not, try to give the word associations: say words that are similar to the analysed one. You may give words in your native language or other languages you speak as well. It may turn out very often that the word exists in other languages, but in a different form. Or it turns out to be a part of another word you know in the foreign language (a derivation).

Well, however you analyse the context or give similar sounding associations, it may happen, that you still don't find out the meaning of a new word or phrase. Don't worry! As I said it is more important to invest your mental and emotional energies in it than to come immediately to the meaning. While repeating and thinking about the word based on the context or word associations, you are building up new neuronal structures. You learn the shape and the sound of the word by this process very thoroughly. Meaning will also come, maybe a bit later. Maybe only in the phase of review when you can look it up in the dictionary. But until then you have worked with the word itself a lot and did a lot to retain it.

If you put your money into your bank account you'll get your interest only later, but without putting it on your account you wouldn't get it at all! Well, the situation in language learning is better, for your investment may be rewarded quite soon.

Some linguists may ask how certain language acquisition hypotheses fit in with this point of autorhythmy technique. Especially those who know Dr. Krashen's hypotheses may put such questions. They'll find the answers at the end of this e-book, where I touch upon the techniques, methods and authors who have shaped autorhythmy (See page 110: Input Hypothesis)

4.MARK the unknown words or phrases!

It is important to mark (underline/ mark with a marker, or highlight in the case of an e-book) the word you were investigating! You may write your notes in the margin of the page as well or in your e-book reader in a pop-up window. Write the important chunks or phrases in the margin or transform them into the first person form: "I..." (See also page 100: *Ten Suggestions for Successful Language Learning*.)

Some ideas for marking in a print book:

- underlining;

- circling of important concepts;

- using different colours;

- asterisk the really useful idioms;

- turn over the page corners where you find words or phrases you want to review more often than usual.

Some ideas for marking and noting in an e-book reader:

- highlighting – you'll find this option in almost every e-book reader;

- noting - in a pop-up window;

- marking the page.

Actually PERM is the basic technique of reading in auto-rhythmy and if you don't want to develop more systematic learning out of reading you may be content to just enjoy learning through reading. But if you want to deepen your knowledge of the recently discovered and learnt new words/phrases you may keep a reader's diary or note them in your note-book. Then undertake reviews at different time intervals.

If you turn out to be a very good reader in a given foreign language, you can use an advanced technique: progressive reading. To be at a good level of reading in a foreign language means that 75-85% of the words of a text are known to you and you understand it globally.

Progressive Reading

Progressive word analysis means that while reading for the first time you attempt to make word analyses as well. In this case you won't need to reread the text - you may do it of course, but it is not necessary.

As a rule: analyse only the words you really think can be useful or those which seem to be interesting to you.

A failure of beginners who start reading books in the foreign language is that they may switch too early to progressive reading. That is to say that they start analysing the unknown words the first time they read a text. Keep in mind: first of all get used to concentrating on the known words, and turn to progressive word analysis only when you feel at ease with the language. Of course this could take time, maybe months or years. Enjoy this process!

How to use the Technique with E-Book Readers?

It is just the same until point 4, when you have to mark the unknown words. If you use a Kindle or other e-book reader, touch the word on your screen, then a window will appear. Don't look at the explanation of the word - in Kindle you'll have a dictionary explanation for the word, or you may install your own dictionary - just mark (highlight) it! You may also add your notes in your e-book reader: the conclusions of your investigation! This can be reviewed separately.

You may need the mark the new words for later review in your note-book!

A very useful option is to search for a word in the whole text and analyse it in a new context. This can be applied when reviewing your notices, too.

Chapter V

After Reading

Exercises after reading are:

- •keeping a reader's diary;

- •and/or noting and listing the new words.

If learning in a systematic way you may use both, but you have to choose at least one of them.

Keeping a Reader's Diary

Keeping a reader's diary can be of great value. You practice writing in this way and you may use the new words you have just discovered. Underline the new words or use a different colour when writing them in your diary. It is also possible to leave some room after the new words to add something to it later. Or simply use the margin for small drawings.

Don't forget to write about your feelings, expectations and emotions you had while reading. You may also put questions and answer them, you also may criticize the author or the characters. All emotions, opinions, remarks will help you remember the plot and the new words.

While you are comprising the summary of the freshly read text you may look at the original, so you won't make many mistakes. That gives you a certain self-confidence which is absolutely vital for a language learner.

A reader's diary is an excellent means of review. It can be more natural then noting and listing the words and phrases. You merge again into the context, this time in your own inner context of the story. You should reread your diary at certain periods of times.

Another possibility is to use a Dictaphone to keep such a diary. It depends on your goals. The latter option allows you to practice speaking and listening to your own voice when reviewing it.

Noting and Listing the New Words – Vocabulary Lists in a Different Way

After you have read a certain part of a book or after the first review you may note the new words or phrases/chunks. Some of them are clear and some still remain unknown to you.

Most of us made vocabulary lists at school: the foreign language words on the left side and the meaning in our native language on the right side. This way of noting and learning new words is quite boring. When I tried to memorize them as a pupil at school I didn't really felt the long-term success. The reason is that it involved only my intellect, not my emotions. Memorizing needs emotions and pictures, too. Therefore we'll need more columns to add to this two column list and involve our emotions as well.

It has to be said that I rarely write down only words on the 'foreign side 'of the list, but rather phrases or a few words (chunks) together. A structure or a chunk may evoke a certain picture, so it is much more concrete than a word on its own.

When noting the new chunks I use a 3- or 4-column list. I write the new words and phrases in the first column. The second column I still leave free or I may draw either simple drawings that describe the meaning or else associative pictures there. Simple drawings don't need to be explained. Don't worry about the perfection of them.

If I have found out the meaning I'll write it in the 3rd column in my native language. If I'm not quite sure about the meaning but I have some suggestions I write question marks behind the "meaning". In the 4th column I may write later idioms from a dictionary that are using the new word analysed.

Associative Drawing

If you have got a difficult word or chunk to remember or you are learning a new language whose structure is totally different from the languages you have already learnt it is useful to draw associative drawings

You draw simple pictures of words of your native language similar to the new one. An example: the Hungarian word 'szék' (chair) you may give a word association 'sake', and draw something maybe linked to "for God's sake" drawing a saintly figure with a halo above his head for God or Good, and he should be pleased (smiling) in the picture. Of course this is only a drawing idea, maybe not very inspired, but it will help you to remember it. You may find out something else. You are once again investing some mental energy. It's not important to be perfect, but try to find something that works for you. The more word associations you find and draw, the better you'll memorize the new words. But be aware that this kind of drawing is only for memorizing the shape of a word that may be difficult for you. The drawing for meaning is different. Draw another picture next to the associative drawing that best depicts the real meaning of the word. In our example you'll easily be able to draw a chair. And make a circle around it. You'll signal by this circle that this is the real meaning of the word and not only an allusive association.

Well I don't use associative drawing for languages I am used to and can speak well. Associative drawing works for me most for languages whose structure and sounds are quite alien to me.

According to Dr. Paul Sulzberger (Victoria University, New Zealand) the more we listen to a language the more our neural structures get developed and we can more easily remember its words and phrases.

"When we are trying to learn new foreign words we are faced with sounds for which we may have absolutely no neural representation. A student trying to learn a foreign language may have few pre-existing neural structures to build on in order to remember the words." (From Phys.org)

Dr Sulzberger looked for ways people could develop these neural structures to make the learning of languages easier. He found that extensive exposure to the language is the key.

Chapter VI

The Review of Words and Phrases

If you want to remember the new words and phrases you have just picked up and analysed from your book, of course you need to review them sometimes. It is more efficient if you review them regularly. There will be words you have easily retained, and words that are more difficult.

In my view reviewing means something different than just repeating the words in an automatic way. Automatic review is unfortunately practiced very often in language learning by reading our vocabulary lists, and it can be one of the motivation killers. Therefore try to avoid or limit automatic repetition. Reviewing must be colourful and varied! Actually its function is to establish the words and phrases to make them available for your everyday use! Actually each time you start reviewing your word and phrase list you should try to do something different from before. This is one of the most important principles of reviewing in autorhythmy.

The following points are suggestions. You may find even other practices to use with your words and phrases in reviewing them. In my experience these are the most proven methods.

1st Review (after roughly 3 days)

Try to remember the context of the phrase or word you marked and imagine that context while "eating" or tasting the word. That means you don't only concentrate on the new words taken out of their context but on the context itself, which is not so fresh after a few days, but even so can generally still be remembered quite easily. If you don't remember it, go through the places again where these words occur in the book and imagine them. In the Kindle reader this means you review your notes, or find the context of your marked words by turning the pages. If you still have words and phrases you haven't found out the meaning of, you may search for other places in the book they occur, and you may analyse them there based on the context. Or look them up in your dictionary on Kindle, which is very easy: you only have to touch the word for a second on the screen and read the description. Only in this phase do we use the dictionary. By this time you'll have become acquainted with the shapes and the pronunciation of the word, and you only need the meaning. If you have got it, write it in the third column of your vocabulary list. Write it in your native language or if you are at an advanced level, write a definition of it in the foreign language.

Putting Questions

In the same session or in one of the following ones you may put questions concerning your new words and phrases. For example your new word or phrase is "Reason it out", you may put the question: "What is he reasoning out?" Your answer could be: "He is reasoning out the new words." Give more answers by adding something to it. "He is reasoning out the new words in the book." Next thing added: "He is reasoning out the new words in the book he is reading." etc. Put at least 2 questions for each new word, and give at least 3 answers to each question and add things to them in order to repeat them.

2nd Review (after 7 days):

Draw simple drawings of the meaning of the word in the second column (of course at those new words and phrases where you didn't draw when you wrote them down for the first time). You may have drawn associative pictures that are supposed to help you get the shapes and forms of the words. Now you should draw alongside this picture another one that you think best demonstrates the meaning - hopefully you'll have enough space to do it! Make simple drawings: basic shapes will do - circles, lines etc. To differentiate between the associative drawings and the ones demonstrating the meaning you may draw a circle around the demonstrating ones. You'll know from the circle that this represents the meaning of the word.

3rd Review (after roughly 10 days)

Go through the list by reading the words or phrases in the third column and name the phrases or words you wrote in the first column without looking at them. If you have got one you don't remember or have difficulties with, write a sample sentence using it. You should take it from your own life. That means you don't just make up a sample sentence, but use something from your own experience. The more you think about a memory that suits the new word, the better the result will be.

Memorable-Phrase Learning

You can use this technique not only for words or phrases you aren't able to memorize but for words and phrases you find in a dictionary. To give you an example: once I stumbled upon a phrase in a dictionary that was new to me and I wanted to memorize it: 'To flip the bird'. I tried to find a memory alluding to this. At first I thought it was going to be hard, as I didn't have memories associated with it. But after a minute or so I remembered that the other day I had stopped my car at some traffic lights. There were pedestrians crossing the street. One started to walk when he already had a red light. He was walking very quietly and peacefully without caring about the cars waiting for him. One driver next to me started tooting very angrily. The pedestrian - in the same quiet manner as he was walking - just flipped the bird to this driver without looking at him at all. This scene was actually very amusing and I started to laugh. So I linked this memory to my new phrase and wrote down: "The pedestrian flipped the bird to the driver."

It's worth searching your memory as it is a very useful investment. But don't overuse this. If you would do this with each new word you find that would be boring after a while. So keep this technique just for those words and phrases that are really hard to remember.

4th Review (after roughly 21 days)

Go through the list looking at the second column and naming both the words in the first column and your sample sentences (if you have got one). If you still have problems remembering any of them, underline them, and use these words to write a simple story. Learn this story by heart and retell it wherever you can (in your car, while travelling or while waiting somewhere).

5th Review – Long-term Review (after 2 months)

Go through the book and remember the context of your marked words. You'll realize that you remember the meaning of your words and phrases. If there are words or phrases you have forgotten or don't remember the meaning of them do something: use memorable-phrase learning or write them on a board or large sheet on your wall!

Well, as a long term review you may also listen to the story (if you have got the audio version of it) at the marked places and imagine the words and the context as you did in the first phase of reading. See the exercises in the following chapter.

Chapter VII

Listening to Audio Books and other Texts

Kató Lomb complained that part of her language learning system, the reading of books in the foreign language, was of little use in acquiring the pronunciation. She listened to radio programmes in different languages to improve her pronunciation and counterbalance the shortcomings of reading. Well, in her early days audio-books weren't available, nor was 'text to speech' software. I am sure she would have used them to great success.

To improve your pronunciation and to develop the articulation of the foreign language you are learning, you have to listen to the language as much as you can, especially to native speakers. If you have the audio version of a book you are reading, listen to it as well.

You may listen to an audio book in one or more of the following ways:

A. While listening to the text read it as well. This helps you get used to the spelling!

B. Listen (without following the written text) to one sentence or short section from the text – stop the device - then clap the rhythm of the heard short section. Do this for a few minutes with the rest of the text. This helps you to stay in the moment of a text as well – you'll see in the next chapter, why is this so important.

C. Do the same as in the previous point, but instead of clapping the rhythm hum the melody of a sentence or short section.

D. Just listen to the text without stopping at each sentence and say the text at the same time. First this could seem difficult but after a few exercises you'll get very good at it. Actually you repeat the spoken text after a very short delay or to put it differently synchronically. This is my favourite exercise when I'm abroad and mimicking silently the speech of native speakers. It helps not only improve the rhythm and melody of the language but makes my vocabulary and grammar more accurate.

E. Another point would be: listen to one sentence of a text and repeat it. Then repeat it again but skip the last word, then repeat it again by skipping the second to last word and so on. When there remains only one word repeat it then add the words to the text until it is whole again.

Well, these exercises should help you to get accustomed to the rhythm and melody of the language and to a certain extent with the articulation of that language. You'll be able to make a distinction between the different sounds of the foreign language. But keep in mind that you also have to practice the pronunciation. You will find very good material for this for different languages. For English you may go to bbc.co.uk where you'll find very good online lessons for pronunciation.

In the next chapter you may read why we don't understand a foreign language we have been learning for years and why the previously suggested exercises will help to deal with this.

Improving your Understanding of Audio Texts and Real Life Speech

Well, you may have also experienced that you've been learning a certain language for several years (or even decades!) and still don't understand the spoken or audio texts, movies, lyrics etc. When listening to it, the language appears to be a heap of meaningless sounds thrown together. Actually that is how for example most Hungarians learning English feel. But it may happen to other nations, too, if their articulation or vocabulary compared to English is quite different.

Even if you are learning a language that belongs to the same language family as your native one, you may experience the above situation!

I experienced the same thing after having studied German for several years very intensively from course books, teachers and by reading novels. I got truly disappointed when at first I didn't understand anything of this language when travelling to Germany. I needed 3 months at that time to get acquainted with the real language (articulatory basis) and to get rid of my artificial image of it that I had built it while learning from course-books. I didn't know about autorhythmy at that time. So I didn't use the practice which helps you only in a few weeks to listen correctly to the spoken language and understand it. Of course there is nothing strange about this and it only occurs if you have been learning the language for a longer period of time. You'll need an adequate vocabulary even to get to this point.

Why does this happen?

Well, when listening to a text or a native speaker, we try to translate the words and phrases, and as we try to remember the meaning of a word, the text goes by and we are just stuck or stumbling with our translation somewhere behind it. Practically we are lost in translation, which means in the jungle of the text. It is no wonder that we feel the text is a collection of nonsensical sounds. To put it differently: we are not in the moment when the text is being spoken - we are not concentrating on the speech itself!

The conclusion is, we have to learn how to be in the moment of a text, in order to understand it.

Let's summarize and see in a bit more detail the reasons why it may be difficult for you to understand the spoken language!

Differences between your articulation and that of the foreign language: You have learnt a language from a course-book, probably with a few pronunciation or comprehension exercises on a tape or CD. One thing is certain: whatever you do while reading as a learner you'll use the articulatory basis of your native language. That's normal.

You won't use exactly the same points of your articulatory organs to pronounce the sounds (mouth, palate, teeth etc.) as required in the foreign language, nor will you be articulating them for the same duration, to say nothing about the precise relation between the sounds. You may be learning a bit of pronunciation of the foreign language. You may know how to pronounce some letters, but that is not enough. You have to get used to the foreign language thoroughly. I can assure you that, as an adult, it never will be 100% , but don't worry, it can be developed to a very high level!

First of all the rhythm and the melody are the most important elements of a language. These are so characteristic, that even if you don't understand or know a language you'll soon recognize it. I am sure if you hear Italian, Japanese, French or any language you have ever identified you will recognize it. You recognize it by its rhythm and melody. These elements may lead to the flow of a conversation. Therefore it is important to practice with the rhythm and melody of a language as well. While our pronunciation in a foreign language can't be perfect when starting to learn the language as an adult, the rhythm and melody of a language can be internalized quite easily. But there is another reason, too, why the rhythm and melody are so important: they may alternate the meaning of a sentence as well.

We have to get the sense to feel it. (We have already learnt about the exercises which help us to do this. See page 66: *Listening to audio books and other texts*)

Immersing yourself in the text! Another reason you may not understand the spoken language is as I stated before, you aren't immersed in it. You stay outside. That means, when you just listen to a text, lyrics, or to someone, you are stuck at the beginning of the sentence because you are trying to decode (convert it to your own articulatory basis and translate it) and miss the rest of the text that is easily passing by while you are involved in time-consuming and unnecessary work.

Have you ever been spoken to in a foreign language by someone, or have you ever tried to get into conversation with someone and understand her or him? Well, you may have experienced success in such cases only if you are immersed in the moment and realize the movements and reactions of your partner. You could only understand them by concentrating on the context, gestures and cir-cumstances, not by translating the words.

But in the case of listening to audio texts and lyrics as well mostly you may try to translate what you hear into your language. And as the text goes on, you miss the rest of it and at the end you may have the sensation that what you have just heard is an unarticulated pile of utterings impossible to understand. Many feel that way when lis-tening to English or other languages.

The key idea and solution is: keep pace with the spoken text and don't translate it, stay in the flow of the speech or text. Be in the moment of the text!

To learn this (keeping pace with the on-going text) first you can concentrate on the rhythm and melody of the language. As in the exercises suggested previously in *Improving your Understanding of Audio Texts and Real Life Speech*) you may clap the rhythm of a sentence or hum its melody after having listened to a short sentence. If you have concentrated on the rhythm and melody and can repeat it by clapping or humming you have merged into the language. But there is another way to achieve this, too.

From a certain point of view it is more practical and you also can use it while listening to an audiotext or conversing with someone. It is about imagining the meaning of the words you understand in the moment when you hear them, then leave your inner pictures pass by as quickly as the text goes on. Just as we do when using the reading technique the rule is: first concentrate on the familiar words.

A good piece of advice is: don't slow down the pace of the text you are listening to (you may have this option on your device). No-one will do it in real life when you are in conversation with someone. You have to improve your being in the moment and in the context exactly as quickly or slowly as a text goes on. You may do it even with very quick audio texts or speakers as well

Here is a brief description of an exercise you could use to improve your ability to do this:

Listen to a text without reading the written text nor stopping the device you are listening to. Just concentrate on the known words to you, just as you did at the 1st point of the reading technique presented in this book. (See page 49: Skip Decoding) Imagine the meaning of the familiar words. Just let your inner pictures flow as the text passes by, and at the next familiar word just do the same. Although you may feel that you understand only a few words, you are able to make out a global understanding of the text. When you learn more vocabulary you'll get better and better at it.

Of course, besides the rhythm and melody you'll need to improve your pronunciation of the special sounds of the foreign language as well by going through pronunciation exercises of the learnt language.

Well, my advice is first of all to practise being in the moment and practise with the rhythm and melody of language - that will best improve your understanding of a language.

Parallel Reading

That could be also fun and it is very efficient. You may be reading a novel both in your native language and in the foreign language. But you may also have the audio version in both languages. So you may combine reading them or listening to it in a parallel way.

Depending on your aims of learning (improving your spelling, gathering vocabulary) you can do the followings:

A. For improving your spelling and understanding use a. or b. as follows:

a. You both listen to the audiobook and read the book aloud in the foreign language using PERM. Make sure you can stop your device when necessary to conduct your investigation!

b. You listen to the audiobook first without reading the print version and picture the words that you understand. Then when getting to the 2nd point of the described technique (EAT the unknown words) you read the print version of the book.

B. For collecting vocabulary

a. You read the novel in your native language first (2 pages or a whole chapter) then read the same in the foreign language with the given technique (PERM).

b.You read the novel in the foreign language (2 pages) with the given technique (PERM) then read it in your native language. When reading in your native language you may compare your conclusions about different words from the previous session.

A rule for A and B is: don't bounce from the foreign language text to your native language text in order to look up the right word in the text. It is tiresome and wouldn't help in the long run. You may only have a look at the words after you have done your investigations, which means you have invested your mental and emotional energy.

Speaking

Well, speaking is the most important skill in language acquisition. Actually most people learn a language to speak it! This skill is also the most complex one. Toddlers don't speak in the first months. They utter their first words when they are between 9-18 months old. Infants only listen until they get used to the language heard from their parents. Language acquisition all in all seems to be a quite long process. It takes about 4-5 years until a child can speak her or his native language quite correctly and with a basic vocabulary of about 1500-2000 words.

Something similar would happen with an adult, if he gets into a foreign language environment. The only difference is that he or she would like to have it all a bit earlier. But even adults shouldn't try speaking until they have got somewhat accustomed to the language.

Remember that language is given to us for speech, for making contact with people. So when you have begun to learn a new language try to speak it as well, but only if you feel comfortable doing so.

An exercise presented in this book previously - which was, by the way, one of the most beloved exercises of Heinrich Schliemann - prepares you for speaking. I'll describe it again:

Listen to a text without stopping it at each sentence and say the text at the same time. At first this could seem difficult but after a few exercises you'll get very good at it. Actually you are repeating the spoken text with a very short delay while you are listening to it, too. Or to put it differently you are speaking synchronically with the speaker.

Heinrich Schliemann listened to sermons in an English church in this way. He imitated the priest while he was talking.

An advanced exercise for practicing speaking is the so-called 'autologue'. I touched upon it before. You speak to yourself, either aloud or silently. You may prepare a topic you are interested in: tell a story of your childhood that you still remember well and may have been influential on your life. Build it up in the foreign language and tell it to yourself. Then retell it when you practise. You should collect several stories like this and learn them by heart in the foreign language.

And perhaps the most important suggestion for speaking is: find people who speak that language and talk to them. You could share your "autologue" stories and you'll soon get very good at telling them.

A Flexible Strategy

A flexible strategy may help if you don't want to get stuck at a seemingly unsuccessful stage. Many learners don't feel they are making progress after studying at school or on courses. Many learners feel after years that their learning of a foreign language was of no use. I meet such people daily. Sometimes I can demonstrate this is not the case. They've been learning a language for years, but something is missing or went wrong. They can't really speak or understand the spoken language. They need the right practice and exercises to develop the missing linguistic skills in the foreign language.

Be sure: nothing happens in vain while you are learning. In my courses I often work with language learners disappointed by language teaching at schools. Though they felt that their language education at school or on courses were of no use, they can understand the spoken or written texts in English after a few weeks. This couldn't happen if their previous learning processes were of no use. Your faculties or skills in the foreign language may appear later, but they will appear, if you don't give up and do the right exercises. Stand your ground and trust in your future progress.

As an autonomous learner you may feel the need to have control of your progress.

You set your goals for the period when you are studying, and take control your progress in the meantime. If something doesn't work in your plan you may change it. The table below may help you to do this. You fill it in, and only have to go through the questions in the table after a week and later to monitor your progress. But "monitoring your progress" means something different from being very strict with yourself and sticking to your plan come what may. On the contrary you should remain flexible and learn from your experiences while studying.

It is important to understand that we don't achieve our goals directly. We achieve them indirectly. This means that during the process there are unforeseeable interactions and discoveries we have to adopt in order to advance.

For example, let's take an example from our recent experience: we'd like to go through a course book. It turns out that going through the course book is not enough. That is OK, but we may stumble as well upon a language club or a site where people gather together to use the foreign language. We'll visit this club or site as well. Or you come across another novel that could be interesting to read in that language. You read the book. We integrate these new things into our learning processes

In his book *Obliquity: Why our goals are best achieved indirectly* John Kay relates that we can't usually achieve our goals by a direct approach but only indirectly. Obliquity is the idea that complex goals are often best pursued indirectly. This is also true in language learning or acquisition. This enables us to understand something more about the subject! So dig your heels in, while staying flexible and open-minded! You may step backwards as well in order to step forward later more quickly!

Plan for a Strategy

The plan below may help you oversee your recent goals and change your exercises if you feel like it. The text in the following plan is just an example, change it according to your needs.

Period of time you can learn intensively (12-14 hours a week): 3rd of Jan. – 3rd of July

Language silence: on weekends, and first two weeks in March

Motivation: I'm going to work abroad; I have to take an exam; I just want to learn the language; It is necessary to speak a foreign language; other:

In-between motivation: language coaching, teacher, talking to others in that language;

The recent situation and setting the goals:

The recent situation: I have got a basic exam, but I don't understand the spoken texts in the foreign language yet, etc. , I know about 700 words (approximately).

Goal for a longer period: I want to read a book; to be able to speak the language; I'd like to understand movies, lyrics in the foreign language; to take a language exam etc.

The goal of the recent learning period: by the end of this learning period I'll add 800 new words to my vocabulary; I will read a book and write down the unknown words; I will watch 3 movies and work with the vocabulary. I'll go through all the lyrics of an album I purchased already!)

Accomplishing: How will I accomplish my goals?: I will read a book or text on the internet by using PERM, by parallel reading. I will learn 7 new words or phrases each day, I will work with my favourite album; I will go through a course book, attend a language course;

When do I have got the time to do it?: Mornings (from 6-8 a.m.) etc. while travelling on the bus, metro etc., 15-20 minutes)

Plan B to 'when do I have the time to do it?'- just if the above plan was missed, write here when you can accomplish it another time:

Fill in your own strategy using the above questions!

Control your Strategy

Have a look at the above strategy once a week, and check whether you were able to accomplish it. If you were successful in accomplishing it congratulate your-self, and be happy about it.

If you weren't successful (which is most likely the first time) alter your plan. Ask yourself what doesn't work for me, and why?

1. I can't be regular in the given period of time. When could I be regular then?

2. The material is boring! Try something else! Change the topic, genre, the book!

3. I don't feel motivated! Find some serious motivation (studying or working in a foreign country, make a jour-ney somewhere where the language is spoken, go to cir-cles where native speakers gather etc.).

Chapter VIII

How to Read a Book - Levels of Reading

There is a very wide and useful literature about reading books. I would recommend to everyone *How to Read a Book* by Mortimer J. Adler and Charles van Doren. The book contains useful information about how to read a book in your native language or a language you are quite familiar with. The book is a must if you are interested in the matter and if you want to benefit to the maximum from reading (mostly practical books) in your native language.

As there are certain differences between the method for reading in foreign languages that I have presented here and Mortimer J. Adler's suggestions, it is important to get acquainted with some terms related to his concept. You can use these suggestions in your native language or a foreign language that you have a really good command of.

According to Adler there are four levels of reading.

1.Elementary level (while learning the letters and developing initial reading skills);

2. Inspectional level of reading (skimming the book);

3. Analytical reading (reading the book in detail);

4. Syntopical level (the reading of several books about one topic or related topics.);

From the viewpoint of our topic 'how to read a book in a foreign language', if you learn a language of which you can read the letters, the 2nd and the 3rd are the most important ones. But let's go through them all from our point of view:

1.Elementary reading is the first level of reading. After you have learnt the letters of a language to recognise them in order to read them and find the meaning in the symbols. You put the questions: What does the sentence mean?

That means while on this level you are developing your basic reading skills. In your native language this happens when you are mostly between 5 and 10 years old. It depends on the method at your school how you get through this phase of learning.

In my experience there are good methods and not really good methods for teaching the basic reading skills. I personally have the experience that where letters are taught in a pictorial and slow way reading will be more effective in the long term. There is no need to hurry. Unfortunately many schools teach children to read quite early.

How to Learn Non-Latin Letters

Even if you are an adult and want to learn a language that uses Non-Latin script, use the pictorial method to learn its letters. Don't try to memorize the new lines of the new letters in an abstract or direct way.

What does this mean?

You draw the new letter using a suitable picture first. Example: The K could be a King walking with his sword holding up. The Hebrew letter 'Mem' could be the entrance of a cave with a twig growing on the left top side.

This way of memorizing the letters seems at first to be time-consuming, as you have to find a picture that best suits the letter and draw it. But in order to learn the letters and get acquainted with them, it'll turn out much more effective than simply trying to memorize the lines of a foreign letter without any picture (that means abstractly without linking it to anything known to you before). In this way you'll learn and remember best those specific letters.

I didn't know about the pictorial method of letter learning when I once started to learn the Katakana and Hiragana (the two syllable-scripts of Japanese using 2 x 72 letters) in an abstract way. The author of the course book suggested that only after having learnt the Katakana and Hiragana should the learner read and learn words and sentences in Japanese. I needed 3 months to recognise these letters and associate them with the appropriate sounds. All this while I had only learnt two sentences in Japanese which I was able to read out with great effort. There wasn't even a chance to learn more as there were no transliterated words or sentences in the book.

After spending 2 hours a day for three months I got bored with these letters and was disappointed. I was even more disappointed when I realised that after a few weeks break, as I hadn't practiced enough before, I could hardly remember the Katakana and Hiragana.

Many years after this adventure learning some Hebrew letters in a pictorial way was much more fun and effective.

And of course after having learnt them you have to practice the letters and forget about the pictures associated with the lines and just stay with the sounds they depict. This happens automatically if you practice enough.

When learning a non-Latin script language make sure that while you are learning the letters you also learn useful phrases in order to merge into the language. Don't wait until you can read the letters. Fortunately there are very good course books with transliterations in them as well.

When you have already learnt a few letters try to transcribe some of them from your native language in the newly learnt letters. Try to find some words in your native language that could be written with them. Or later on it is fun to see your name or the names of your friends and relatives in a new script. This is the quickest way to get accustomed to the new letters.

Further Levels of Reading

Another level of reading in your native language according to Mortimer J. Adler is inspectional reading. It means that you can read now well (you have already learnt the letters and developed your basic reading skills) and that you can now "inspect" the book, getting information about it and learning its subject. You put the question 'What is the book about?' You are inspecting a book in the library or bookshop to decide whether it would be of interest to you or not. This is the first phase of inspectional reading. But you can inspect it further when taking it home to get basic information about it. Actually when reading in a foreign language we first do inspectional reading as well. We might also call this pre-reading.

According to Adler you can do inspectional reading in two steps.

Some of the following points are important to employ also when reading in a foreign language but there are some that would be counterproductive to employ.

The First Step - Systematic Skimming:

- you are getting an idea about the subject of the book by looking at the cover and title page, or reading its preface;

- you study the table of contents to have a general idea about the book's structure. Mortimer J. Adler says: "Use it as you would a road map before taking a trip";

- study the index and estimate the range of topics covered. When you see terms that seem crucial, look them up, at least some;

- read the publisher's blurb;

- look at the chapters that seem pivotal to its argument. (these chapters probably will have summary statements in their opening or closing pages. Read these statements carefully;

- finally turn the pages, dipping in here and there, reading one or more paragraphs: above all read the last two to three pages or the epilogue;

All these points would work in our case (reading in a foreign language) only for expository or practical books. But if you follow my suggestion to read a novel that really interests you (detective story, pulp fiction etc.) in a foreign language don't follow the last two points. Looking up the end of a crime novel for example, would kill your motivation to read it to the end. Anyway the above points are good to know about and to practice in the case of practical works of all kinds, be they in a foreign or in your native language.

In The Second Step Of Inspectional Reading:

you read through the book without bothering about sentences or words you don't understand. Actually this is one of the keys that enable us to get to the global meaning of a text. We were taught to concentrate on things we don't understand and to look them up in the dictionary, but this is false and we have to accustom ourselves to another way of getting to the meaning of a text.

Analytical Reading

This is the next level of reading. You have learnt about the subject of your book on the previous level. Now you have to go into details. Well, analytical reading doesn't only mean that you read the book thoroughly from the beginning to the end but it involves your intense activity. You take notes, put questions and find the answers to them. You'll have to find keywords and key propositions of the author. You'll have to interpret the book's content as well as to come to terms with the author or to criticize him.

In autorhythmy we also do something similar. But our concentration in this phase will be on the unknown words we analyse based on the context and previously gained global understanding of the text when we concentrated on the familiar words alone.

To put it differently, on this level you read the book until it becomes your own! How far it becomes your own depends on the intensity with which you work at it.

Syntopical reading

is the most complex and systematic level of reading. You read several books about one topic and place them in a relation to one another. It is not about mere comparison. The reader on this level is able to construct an analysis that is in none of the books being read. If you are interested in this level and really want to get most out of your books, read the book by Mortimer J. Adler.

By presenting in brief these levels of reading set by Mortimer J. Adler I only wanted to show you that reading can be done systematically and it is important to do it so if we want to learn something new.

For the reading technique of autorhythmy see page 45: *The Technique – PERM.*

Chapter IX

The Background to Auto-rhythmy – Polyglots

Now let's have a look at different personalities and methods that influenced autorhythmy. I heartily recommend you to read about the personalities mentioned here, as their lives and activities could be very inspiring for every language learner. And If you are a language teacher even your pupils or students would benefit from their biographies. I also recommend you to read about the methods described in this chapter (PLA and the Waldorf School).

I hope that not only language teachers would enjoy reading about the personalities and techniques following, as they represent something very different from the usual techniques of language learning.

I would like to mention that autorhythmy is a coherent system that has its own goals for which it uses relevant exercises. These exercises weren't simply thrown together but they serve certain purposes.

The exercises of the following polyglots or systems are in some way related to each other or to autorhythmy as they use, besides emotional involvement of the language learners, the rhythm and melody, too.

The Waldorf School

At the beginning of this book I touched upon the notion that the rhythm and the melody of the language plays a great role in teaching at a Waldorf School. In order to give you a picture of what is going on in a Waldorf School environment I suggest you read the following article written by me that first appeared in June 2009, in Humanising Language Teaching Magazine.

Teaching the small ones

A few years ago I had a busy and exciting summer. I was preparing for teaching English and Spanish to primary classes. After having teaching experience only with adults this was a big challenge for me. In fact that was the reason I accepted the job. I learnt to play the flute, different verses, nursery rhymes, songs, clapped the rhythm of songs and tried to find out how to stand in front of small children and how to introduce a song, a poem, a tale or whatever, and what is going to happen in a lesson of 25-30 minutes. I thought before it would never happen in my life to teach foreign languages to small children. The world of children is a different world, you have to talk to them in a different way. Therefore it is a big but very nice challenge to change yourself into a child, or put it more precisely, it is a big but very nice challenge to reawaken the child living in us!

The most important argument on the side of early foreign language learning at school is that children grow into another language merely through their ability to mime the teacher and they develop speech ability in a foreign language, too, in a period when their speech organs are very flexible to form the sounds of another language.

Alright, that sounds good, but what can I do with children in the lesson? And above all, I couldn't use books, tapes or videos as a rule at this school! The answer is in fact surprisingly simple and is based on a very interesting phenomenon that mostly remains unconsidered and unused in traditional schools at lower classes. A small child, if untouched by such modern devices as computers and the television, feels a basic urge to mimic the adults in their environment – I have to add, that even children who get in touch quite early with the technical world of today will feel this urge if they have the possibility to mimic someone within the frame of a lesson. The teacher doesn't have to do anything else than stand in front of the pupils and they will copy his movements his gestures and words, speech, pronunciation. Mimicry is an important element of life for the children until they lose their milk teeth. But even in the first years of school this is relatively strong enough to be of use for the teacher. In a lesson like this even the intellectually mediocre or feeble children can have a fairly good achievement and can find joy in foreign languages.

It should be mentioned that in fact what is going on here is not mimicking in a strict sense, but synchronic singing and moving with the teacher

De facto the children are able to copy me in a fraction of a second. Thus the children experience the atmosphere of a language through the movements of the teacher, through the songs and verses.

In that summer I had a bit of headache, as I was only theoretically prepared to do all that, even though I had visited some lessons of the class teacher. I couldn't imagine that these little ones (class 1 and 2) will copy me in the same way in the English and Spanish lessons as they did with their class teacher. And I had another problem that most adults experience when learning rhymes songs and verses. I couldn't learn so many by heart as I imagined to be necessary to fill a year's lessons with. So I decided to learn some of them for the first 3-4 weeks and then gradually learn others as well, enabling me to be one or two steps ahead of the children. But in practice it was different. You don't have to perform a concert or a show to the children with your repertoire, you are practising language, you are playing with them and the language of course. Things were much easier and instead of headaches I enjoyed the lessons and being with the children!

We could repeat a verse for example several times; the first time in a normal voice, then in a lower voice and finally only to ourselves. In the first lesson I realized that children would like to have the thing I had brought along which made an allusion to the meaning of a text we were singing or reciting while making certain movements that described the text as well. We didn't translate anything, and I used the mother tongue very rarely. For each song, verse or tale I had an object with me which was referred to in the text. The children were eager to get in their hands the lamp, the branch or maybe, in Autumn, a yellow leaf when singing, reciting or moving with me. But we had only one thing for each song or verse, so we had to repeat the texts several times, as almost each child wanted once to hold the thing in his or her hands when acting. So we managed to repeat a song or verse for 7 or 9 times (I usually got bored of it by the 7th or 8th time, but not the children. They couldn't get enough of the actual thing I usually took out from the English box or Spanish sack. Later on I usually repeated a song or verse for maximum 6 times and tried to amuse myself by adding something to it at each time. Of course we did lots of things beside this, we played different games, or I told tales to them. But I was very grateful, as one of my greatest troubles was solved by this kind of meaningful repetition: how I could learn hundreds of verses. That was not necessary, 10-12 verses, 15-20 songs, 3-5 games will do for a year!

One of the greatest experiences I had was while introducing a new song in my 3rd year of teaching small children. This happened in the first class. I usually introduced a new song by its melody. I played it on the flute then we just sang the melody humming without words holding each other's hand and wandering in a circle. Then at the 3rd or 4th time I sang the text as well. The children usually looked very attentively at me and tried to sing along. Of course they usually hummed and tried to mime the movements of my mouth and get out the same sounds that I did. But this time there was a little girl next to me holding my hand who sang very clearly the song we sang for the first time. I thought she had a brother or sister in one of the upper classes, whom I may have taught this song to, and she may have learnt it from him or her, or probably from a playmate from a higher class. But it turned out that she hadn't got a sister or a brother and she hadn't heard this song at all before. I was astonished by this fact and I didn't really know how this could happen, and even now I am quite unsure about a precise explanation. Finally I decided to explain this phenomena partially by the synchrony studied by W.S Condon and W. D. Ogston in the US in the sixties. These two scholars studied communication between people, recording on film what they do when talking to each other. They filmed the movements with 100 slides a second and after studying their movements they concluded, when people talk to each other they mirror in a certain way each other's micro-movements. In a certain way this is a kind of mimicry of another person. This happens in a fraction of a second and serves the understanding of each other's messages. The power of synchrony appears in each human being right after birth. I think I could recognize synchrony in an active form with that very young lady in my lesson!

Even if there is a great likelihood that you will get frustrated about how to do it in the right way, I recommend teaching young children to every teacher, as this is one of the greatest possibilities to get rare insights into how language is being acquired, and sometimes into how language itself is being created. Whatever strategies you find to solve your problems arising when teaching young people in primary classes, there are two things to be borne in mind above all: the first is the being of child in front of you and the second is the child within your own self!"

Kató Lomb

I stumbled upon Kató Lomb's book in a public library by chance in Hungary, when I was looking for practical techniques for learning languages. Her book has been translated into English since then: (*Polyglot, How I Learn languages*. Kató Lomb 2008, TESL-EJ, Berkeley & Kyoto):

The conference interpreter and translator, Kató Lomb worked with 16 languages, but in all she learnt about 26 or 27. In her book she describes her techniques of learning languages in a very entertaining way, from which the most amazing and unbelievable to me was reading books in foreign languages without a dictionary. She used this method even at the beginning of learning a language. I am thankful I read her book. It helped me enter Teacher Training College and to graduate as a Language Teacher for German and Rumanian. Since then I have also taught Spanish and English at different schools and in private lessons. Furthermore I started to learn another 11 languages, of course using mainly the principles of Kató Lomb and autorhythmy.

Wikipedia says about her:

"Kató Lomb (Pécs, February 8, 1909 – Budapest, June 9, 2003) was a Hungarian interpreter, translator, language genius and one of the first simultaneous interpreters in the world.

Originally she graduated in physics and chemistry, but her interest soon led her to languages. Native in Hungarian, she was able to interpret fluently in nine or ten languages (in four of them even without preparation), and she translated technical literature and read belles-lettres in six languages. She was able to understand journalism in further eleven languages. As she put it, altogether she earned money with sixteen languages (BULGARI-

AN, CHINESE, DANISH, ENGLISH, FRENCH, GERMAN, HEBREW, ITALIAN, JAPANESE, LATIN,   POLISH,   ROMANIAN, RUSSIAN, SLOVAK, SPANISH, UKRAINIAN).   SHE LEARNED THESE LANGUAGES MOSTLY BY SELF-EFFORT, AS AN AUTODIDACT. Her aims to acquire these languages were most of all practical, to satisfy her interest.

According to her own account, her long life was highlighted not primarily by the command of languages but the actual study of them. Through her books, published in Hungarian in several editions as well as in some other languages, interviews (in print and on the air) and conversations, she tried to share this joy with generations. (Egy tolmács a világ körül, "An interpreter around the world").”...

Her language learning method and principles

Her keyword was most of all interest: the word, coming from Latin interesse (originally meaning "to be between"), has a double meaning, referring to the material profit or the mental attraction, together: motivation. This means that I can answer these questions: "How much am I interested in it? What do I want with it? What does it mean for me? What good is it for me?" She didn't believe in the so-called language talent. She tended to express the language skill with a fraction, with motivation in the numerator (through which we can pinch off some ten minutes a day even with the busiest job), and inhibition in the denominator (the fear of starting to speak, of being clumsy, of being laughed at). In her conviction, the stronger the motivation is within us, and the more we can put aside inhibition, the sooner we can take possession of the language.

Even she was bored with the fabricated dialogues of coursebooks, so her favourite method was to obtain an original novel in a language completely unknown to her, whose topic she personally found interesting (a detective story, a love story, or even a technical description would do), and that was how she deciphered, unravelled the basics of the language: the essence of the grammar and the most important words. She didn't let herself be set back by rare or complicated expressions: she skipped them, saying: what is important will sooner or later emerge again and will explain itself if necessary. ("It's much more of a problem if the book becomes flavourless in our hands due to the many interruptions than not learning if the inspector watches the murderer from behind a blackthorn or a hawthorn.") So we don't really need even a dictionary: it only spoils our mood from the joy of reading and discovering the texts. In any case, what we can remember is what we have figured out ourselves. /(From Wikipedia)

I also would like to quote her 10 suggestions for successful language learning from her book (*Polyglot*, Kató Lomb 2008, TESL-EJ, Berkeley Kyoto):

Ten Suggestions For Successful Language Learning.

I.

Spend time tinkering with the language every day. If time is short, try at least to produce a 10-minute monologue. Morning hours are especially valuable in this respect: the early bird catches the word!

II.

If your enthusiasm for studying flags too quickly, don't force the issue but don't stop altogether either. Move to some other form of studying, e.g., instead of reading, listen to the radio; instead of writing a composition, poke about in the dictionary, etc.

III.

Never learn isolated units of speech; rather, learn them in context.

IV.

Write phrases in the margins of your text and use them as "prefabricated elements" in your conversations.

V.

Even a tired brain finds rest and relaxation in quick, impromptu translations of billboard advertisements flashing by, of numbers over doorways, of snippets of overheard conversations, etc., just for its own amusement.

VI.

Memorize only that which has been corrected by a teacher. Do not keep studying sentences you have written that have not been proofread and corrected so mistakes don't take root in your mind. If you study on your own, each sentence you memorize should be kept to a size that precludes the possibility of errors.

VII.

Always memorize idiomatic expressions in the first person singular. For example, "I am only pulling your leg."

VIII.

A foreign language is a castle. It is advisable to besiege it from all directions: newspapers, radio, movies that are not dubbed, technical or scientific papers, textbooks, and the visitor at your neighbour's.

IX.

Do not let the fear of making mistakes keep you from speaking, but do ask your conversation partner to correct you. Most importantly, don't get peeved if he or she actually obliges you—a remote possibility, anyway.

X.

Be firmly convinced that you are a linguistic genius. If the facts demonstrate otherwise, heap blame on the pesky language you aim to master, your dictionaries, or this book—but not on yourself.

Heinrich Schliemann

After an adventurous life of living in different countries he became rich and finally dedicated himself to archaeology. As he was captivated in his youth by Homer's works, the Odyssey and the Iliad, he dreamed of finding Troy. He fulfilled his dream. He was an autonomous and very practical language learner who enjoyed learning. To be autonomous in language learning means that he decided how to learn and what to learn. As he was interested in ancient Greek mythology, he read books about it.

One of his favourite books was *The Adventures of Telemachus*, which he read or listened to in different languages.

He realized very well that reading only doesn't help in speaking and understanding the spoken language itself, so he hired people to read aloud to him.

Another technique of his was to mimic speakers. In the Netherlands where he was washed up, after the foundering of the ship he had boarded to emigrate to America, he used to go to the English church and listen to the Holy Service there. He repeated the text right after the priest, almost in synchrony with him.

Wikipedia says about him:

"Heinrich Schliemann was a German businessman and amateur archaeologist, and an advocate of the historical reality of places mentioned in the works of Homer. His work lent weight to the idea that Homer's *Iliad* and Virgil's *Aeneid* reflect actual historical events.

He was born in Germany (Neubukow, Mecklenburg-Schwerin) in 1822. His father, Ernst Schliemann, was a Protestant minister.

Heinrich's later interest in history was initially encouraged by his father, who had schooled him in the tales of the Iliad and the Odyssey and had given him a copy of Ludwig Jerrer's *Illustrated History of the World* for Christmas in 1829. Schliemann later claimed that at the age of 8, he had declared he would one day excavate the city of Troy.

However, Heinrich had to transfer to the Realschule (vocational school) after his father was accused of embezzling church funds and had to leave that institution in 1836 when his father was no longer able to pay for it. His family's poverty made a university education impossible, so it was Schliemann's early academic experiences that influenced the course of his education as an adult. He wanted to return to the educated life, to reacquire and explore the interests he had been deprived of in childhood. In his archaeological career, however, there was often a division between Schliemann and the educated professionals.

At age of 14 Heinrich became an apprentice at Herr Holtz's grocery in Fürstenberg. One story has it that his passion for Homer was born when he heard a drunkard reciting it at the grocer's. He labored for five years, until he was forced to leave because he burst a blood vessel lifting a heavy barrel.[4] In 1841, Schliemann moved to Hamburg and became a cabin boy on the *Dorothea,* a steamer bound for Venezuela. After twelve days at sea, the ship foundered in a gale. The survivors washed up on the shores of the Netherlands.[5] Schliemann became a messenger, office attendant, and later, a bookkeeper in Amsterdam. On March 1, 1844, 22-year old Schliemann took a position with B. H. Schröder & Co., an import/export firm. In 1846 the firm sent him as a General Agent to St. Petersburg. In time, Schliemann represented a number of companies. He continued to nourish a passion for the Homeric story and an ambition to become a great linguist. He learned Russian and Greek, employing a system that he used his entire life to learn languages— Schliemann claimed that it took him six weeks to learn a language and wrote his diary in the language of whatever country he happened to be in.

By the end of his life, he could converse in English, French, Dutch, Spanish, Portuguese, Swedish, Polish, Italian, Greek, Latin, Russian, Arabic, and Turkish as well as German. Schliemann's ability with languages was an important part of his career as a businessman in the importing trade."

Cardinal Giuseppe Mezzofanti

He is a legendary figure from the 18th and 19th centuries. He was said to speak (in all including dialects) 102 languages. As a priest, Mezzofanti used to visit the soldiers wounded in the battles near Bologna (his hometown) in 1799-1800. He asked these soldiers gathered together from different places from Europe to repeat the well-known prayers he was familiar with in their own language. He learnt these by heart and made an analysis of the text right afterwards while walking home from the hospital. He deciphered the words and worked out the rules of a given language in this way. He acquired the language directly and picked up the pronunciation very accurately. He could speak, for example, 6 Hungarian dialects.

In order to practise the language he met people who spoke that language and he used to read biblical texts to increase his vocabulary in that language.

The Catholic Encyclopeadia says of him:

A cardinal, the greatest of polyglots, born 19 September, 1774; died 15 March, 1849. He was the son of a poor carpenter of Bologna. In the Scuole Pie, besides the classical languages, he learned Spanish, German, Mexican, and some South American dialects from ex-Jesuits who had been exiled from America. To his great love of study he added a prodigious memory, so that at the age of twelve years he was able to begin the three years course of philosophy, which he closed with a public disputation. His theological studies were completed with no less distinction, at an age at which he could not yet be ordained; consequently he devoted himself to the study of Oriental languages; and in 1797 he was appointed to the chair of Hebrew at the University of Bologna, and ordained a pries.

[…]After the battles of 1799 and of 1800, the hospitals of Bologna were crowded with wounded and sick of almost all the nationalities of Europe, and Mezzofanti in giving religious assistance to the unfortunate seized the opportunity of perfecting his knowledge of the languages which he had already studied, as well as of learning new ones.

In 1803 he was appointed assistant in the library of the Institute, and later, professor of Hebrew and of Greek at the university, which relieved him financially. In 1806, he refused an invitation of Napoleon to establish himself at Paris.

[…]In 1815, he became librarian of the university, and occupied his chair once more. Besides the study of languages, to which he gave many hours of the day and night, he devoted himself to the study of ethnology, archæology, numismatics, and astronomy. Moreover, he performed the offices of his holy ministry, and was commonly called the confessor of foreigners.

In 1831 he was among the deputies who went to ask the pope's forgiveness, in the name of the city of Bologna, for the rebellion of that year, and the pope, repeating Pius VII's invitation of 1814 requested Mezzofanti to remain at Rome and place his learning directly at the service of the Holy See, an invitation which the modest priest, this time, accepted, after long resistance; soon he received the title of Domestic Prelate, and a canonry at Santa Maria Maggiore, which was changed, later, for one at St. Peter's. At Rome, also, he took advantage of opportunities to practice the languages that he had acquired, and to master new ones and in order to learn Chinese he went to the Capodimonte college for foreign missions, at Naples.

In 1833, he was named Custodian-in-Chief of the Vatican Library, and Consultor of the Congregation for the correction of the Liturgical Books of Oriental Rites, of which he became Prefect. On 12 February, 1838, he was created cardinal under the title of St. Onofrio al Gianicolo; he was also a member of the congregations of the Propaganda, of Rites, of the Index, and of the Examination of Bishops.

The events of 1848 undermined his already enfeebled health, and a combination of pneumonia and gastric fever put an end to his life. He was buried without pomp in a modest tomb of his titular church, over which a monument was raised in 1885.

According to Russell, Cardinal Mezzofanti spoke perfectly thirty-eight languages, among which were: biblical and rabbinic Hebrew, Arabic, Chaldean, Coptic, Armenian, ancient and modern, Persian, Turkish, Albanian, Maltese, Greek, ancient and modern, Latin, Italian, Spanish, Portuguese, French, German, English, Illyrian, Russian, Polish, Bohemian, Magyar, Chinese, Syriac, Gees, Amharic, Hindustani, Guzerati, Basque, Wallachian, and Californian; he spoke thirty other languages, less perfectly, and fifty dialects of the languages mentioned above.

His knowledge of these languages was intuitive, rather than analytic, he left no scientific works, although some studies in comparative linguistics are to be found among his manuscripts, which he left, in part, to the municipal library, and in part to the library of the University of Bologna."

Stephen Krashen's Hypotheses

Stephen Krashen (University of Southern California) is an expert in the field of linguistics, specializing in theories of language acquisition and development. Dr. Krashen has published more than 350 papers and books on second-language acquisition and bilingual education.

Krashen also promotes the use of free voluntary reading during second-language acquisition, which "is the most powerful tool we have in language education, first and second".

Well, he is also a fan of Kató Lomb just like I am! He described his meeting with Kató Lomb in a letter written to us for the annual anniversary of her birthday which is celebrated each year in the National Library of Foreign Languages in Budapest.

Stephen Krashen has contributed to language learning and acquisition research with important hypotheses.

His hypotheses amongst others are: the acquisition-learning hypothesis, the input hypothesis, the monitor hypothesis, the affective filter, and the natural order hypothesis.

I'll touch upon the first four of these and describe how they apply to the reading technique of autorhythmy. Although the natural order hypothesis is also important and interesting we won't really experience it while reading or listening.

Acquisition-Learning Hypothesis

This theory is at the core of modern language acquisition theory, and is the most fundamental of Krashen's hypotheses.

Well, I was astonished many years ago, when I first heard about the distinction between language acquisition and learning. Why is that important? Can we really make a distinction between them?

Let's define them in brief.

Language learning is a conscious process, just like what usually happens in schools! We learn rules, do drills and tests, homework etc.

Language acquisition on the other hand is subconscious learning, just as children learn when learning their native language. They don't do drills in classical terms but they play, interact, make up verses and do things instinctively.

This distinction makes things clearer. Therefore we as learners should acquire a language as much as possible. That is to say we should do things that help us get used to the language unconsciously (it is not about learning in our sleep or such obscure ways!). Of course we have to learn also, but we should try to get into situations where our subconscious is supposed to do the work.

Reading a book in the foreign language can be both a matter of language acquisition and language learning, as there are many things practiced unconsciously when reading, and there are conscious processes as well.

We don't need to look up each word in the dictionary to understand a text (repeated unconscious process). Beside this we do word investigation which is, on the other hand, a very conscious part of the technique.

Krashen says:

"Language acquisition does not require extensive use of conscious grammatical rules, and does not require tedious drills."

"Acquisition requires meaningful interaction in the target language - natural communication - in which speakers are concerned not with the form of their utterances but with the messages they are conveying and understanding."

Input Hypothesis

"If I represents previously acquired linguistic competence and extra-linguistic knowledge, the hypothesis claims that we move from i to i+1 by understanding input that contains i+1. Extra-linguistic knowledge includes our knowledge of the world and of the situation, that is, the context. The +1 represents new knowledge or language structures that we should be ready to acquire.

[…] It must be stressed however, that just any input is not sufficient, the input received must be comprehensible." (From Wikipedia)

In the reading technique described in this book it is the context we understand based on our previous knowledge and linguistic competence and +1 is defined actually by ourselves, as we concentrate on the context we understand. And when reading the text for the second time we choose certain new words or phrases to investigate them and find out their meaning based on the context or through association. Well now the question arises whether these new words we investigate are comprehensible and really represent +1 level.

Actually when investigating the new words and phrases we check whether they are at +1 level. Those we are able to understand based on the context or based on association are at this level for sure. And those which aren't understandable for us are a higher level compared to our linguistic competence and knowledge. The more comprehensible input we have in a book the more successful we'll be in learning by reading it.

According to Krashen, there are three corollaries to his theory.

Talking (output) is not practicing:

Krashen stresses yet again that speaking in the target language does not result in language acquisition. Although speaking can indirectly assist in language acquisition, the ability to speak is not the cause of language learning or acquisition. Instead, comprehensible output is the result of language acquisition.

When enough comprehensible input is provided, i+1 is present: that is to say, that if language models and teachers provide enough comprehensible input, then the structures that acquirers are ready to learn will be present in that input. According to Krashen, this is a better method of developing grammatical accuracy than direct grammar teaching.

The teaching order is not based on the natural order: Instead, students will acquire the language in a natural order by receiving comprehensible input."

(from Wikipedia)

"The best methods are therefore those that supply 'comprehensible input' in low-anxiety situations, containing messages that students really want to hear. These methods do not force early production in the second language, but allow students to produce when they are 'ready', recognizing that improvement comes from supplying communicative and comprehensible input, and not from forcing and correcting production."

(from:www.sdkrashen.com/Principles_and_Practice/007. html)

Stephen Krashen

Well, reading for ourselves is a low-anxiety situation containing enough comprehensible input!

Monitor Hypothesis

"The monitor hypothesis asserts that a learner's learned system acts as a monitor to what they are producing. In other words, while only the acquired system is able to produce spontaneous speech, the learned system is used to check what is being spoken.

112

Before the learner produces an utterance, he or she internally scans it for errors, and uses the learned system to make corrections. Self-correction occurs when the learner uses the Monitor to correct a sentence after it is uttered. According to the hypothesis, such self-monitoring and self-correction are the only functions of conscious language learning.

The Monitor model then predicts faster initial progress by adults than children, as adults use this 'monitor' when producing L2 (target language) utterances before having acquired the ability for natural performance, and adult learners will input more into conversations earlier than children.

Three conditions for use of the monitor:

According to Krashen, for the Monitor to be successfully used, three conditions must be met:

1. The acquirer/learner must know the rule.
This is a very difficult condition to meet because it means that the speaker must have had explicit instruction on the language form that he or she is trying to produce.

2. The acquirer must be focused on correctness.

He or she must be thinking about form, and it is difficult to focus on meaning and form at the same time.

3. The acquirer/learner must have time to use the monitor.
Using the monitor requires the speaker to slow down and focus on form.

Difficulties using the monitor:

There are many difficulties with the use of the monitor, making the monitor rather weak as a language tool.

Knowing the rule: this is a difficult condition to meet, because even the best students do not learn every rule that is taught, cannot remember every rule they have learned, and can't always correctly apply the rules they do remember. Furthermore, every rule of a language is not always included in a text nor taught by the teacher

Having time to use the monitor: there is a price that is paid for the use of the monitor- the speaker is then focused on form rather than meaning, resulting in the production and exchange of less information, thus slowing the flow of conversation. Some speakers over-monitor to the point that the conversation is painfully slow and sometimes difficult to listen to.

The rules of language make up only a small portion of our language competence: Acquisition does not provide 100% language competence. There is often a small portion of grammar, punctuation, and spelling that even the most proficient native speakers may not acquire. While it is important to learn these aspects of language, since writing is the only form that requires 100% competence, these aspects of language make up only a small portion of our language competence." (from Wikipedia)

Affective Filter Hypothesis

"The affective filter is an impediment to learning or acquisition caused by negative emotional ("affective") responses to one's environment. It is a hypothesis of second-language acquisition theory, and a field of interest in educational psychology.

According to the affective filter hypothesis, certain emotions, such as anxiety, self-doubt, and mere boredom interfere with the process of acquiring a second language. They function as a filter between the speaker and the listener that reduces the amount of language input the listener is able to understand. These negative emotions prevent efficient processing of the language input. The hypothesis further states that the blockage can be reduced by sparking interest, providing low-anxiety environments and bolstering the learner's self-esteem.

According to Krashen (1982), there are two prime issues that prevent the lowering of the affective filter. The first is not allowing for a silent period (expecting the student to speak before they have received an adequate amount of comprehensible input according to their individual needs). The second is correcting their errors too early on in the process." (from Wikipedia)

The affective filter is lowered greatly by reading a book that we are really interested in - or reading a book that we really loved in our native language is also a proven way to lessen the affective filter!

Bernard Dufeu's PLA (Psychodrama for Language Acquisition)

When I began to develop Autorhythmy for myself and my students based, amongst others, on Kato Lomb's approach, Mario Rinvolucri (Pilgrims, UK) recommended to me Bernard Dufeu's book *Teaching Myself.* The book is a good base and much much more for any passionate language teacher be she or he experienced or not.

I would like to mention a few of the most important ideas about the method documented in Dufeu's book

1.The importance of change in the language teaching system from the pedagogy of having to the pedagogy of being: the method of Bernard Dufeu, the Psychodramaturgy for Language Acquisition, ends with any authoritative teaching and changes the system from the bottom.

2.The acquisition of correct pronunciation is crucial from the very beginning and is based on getting acquainted with the prosodic characteristics of the language, rhythm, melody and pronunciation. The written or read work is based on this.

3.The spontaneous development of the curriculum within certain frames (exercises of Psychodrama and Dramaturgy) is mostly based on the speech intentions of the protagonists (learners); there is no previously written material at the beginning. This allows a very deep involvement in the language as the curriculum is being developed while the protagonists interact with the trainer and with each other in some dramatic situations.

4.Skills like empathy, receptivity, auditory memory, or social skills are developed in the course as well and have the same importance as writing, reading, comprehension, and speaking, as these latter are only one side of the coin and not the only skills on which should be concentrated in the language class. Developing these skills greatly supports language learning.

5.Tales and myths can help language learning by their significant functions as they put us in contact us with our deepest psychological levels.

6.Grammar is not in an "input" but in an "output" position. The rules will be discovered by the participants. Correctness is important, but it is subordinated to expression.

I don't think that all ideas from above should be presented in detail in this book, but some, may be the strangest ones should be explained:

2. The acquisition of a correct pronunciation is crucial and is based on getting acquainted with the prosodic characteristics of the language such as rhythm, melody and pronunciation, from the very beginning. The written or read work is based on this.

The trainer explains the exercise for the group on the very first day within the frames of a warming up exercise that prepares for the main exercise. Explanation is needed, as this exercise may be very different form the usual ones done by the participants in previous courses. The animator explains that it is very important to first learn the rhythm, melody and sounds of a language because this greatly helps the understanding, then he says a sequence which is repeated by the group in chorus. This helps the pupils get into contact with the prosodic elements of the language. The trainer accompanies his words with gestures as well so it leads the participants toward a global understanding rather than an understanding of individual units.

Rhythm: to encounter a foreign language is at first like experiencing a new rhythm. The rhythm provides the structural framework into which melodies and sounds can fit. Participants are helped to recognize what is specific about their own rhythm. Then they begin exercises based on natural rhythms found in the foreign language.

The function of intonation is to help a person's spoken words to resonate and live and to express all the elements of the message, that is to say, its emotional and personal as well as its intellectual components. Memory is stimulated when rhythm and melody are taken into account. The language practised in the exercises of PLA is full of such characteristics and, being personal, it works its way into the body and mind more easily so that it is progressively assimilated without being consciously learnt by heart.

Learners often tend to speak lifelessly in the foreign language, which reflects the fact that it has been taught to them throughout their school lives with its emotional content removed. They need help to rediscover the expressiveness of the sounds in the language.

In PLA the protagonists are sensitized to vocal nuances. Participants are made aware of their body's zones of sound resonance, the effects of their vibration, and their influence on breathing movements.

3.The curriculum is developed spontaneously while the trainer gives certain frames and proposes some exercises. Self-expression is central to language acquisition. Learners should be the authors of their own speech: everyone has something to communicate, real or imaginary, directed to others or to himself or herself. The message is inseparable from the people who give it sense and value.

There are many exercises that allow the participants to create their own speech intentions; of course they are helped by the animator. Dufeu uses the techniques of psychodrama such as doubling, mirroring and role change. In one of the exercises, for example, the trainer sits behind the protagonist in the middle of the group. The participant says a word or if she or he is an advanced student, a sentence three times with different intonations. Through the intonation the participant may express different meanings. The trainer listens to the intonation very carefully and pays particular attention to the paraverbal elements joining the speech. After identifying himself or herself with the protagonist the trainer extends the words of the protagonist by saying sentences referring to the previous words or sentences of the protagonist. The words of the trainer are spontaneous and simple coherent ones. They go around the protagonist's words with synonyms. The animator takes care to respect the protagonist's personal space. The animator focuses on the protagonist, if she or he accepts his sequences or not. In this way a complex text comes about that can be developed further and further.

4. A central pedagogic objective in PLA is to continue to contribute to the personal development of the protagonist generally. Encouragement of his or her aptitudes, attitudes, and types of behaviour which will advance the essential components of communication-receptiveness, and capacity for expression. The exercises in the context of an appropriate setting for acquisition and learning, develop receptiveness, i.e. listening skills, openness, empathy, sensitivity towards oneself and others, intellectual development, observation skills, synthetic and analytical processes, and non-stressful concentration. There are two interlinked areas for developing a capacity for expression: the linguistic and the personal.

Linguistic development includes a broadening of the capacity for rhythmic and melodic reproduction which assumes acquiring breathing and vocal techniques, a reinforcement of our capacity for synthesising information in a new setting, of association, creativity, and a willingness to experiment.

Personal development includes developing spontaneity, creativity, willingness to become involved, of expressing ourselves as individuals, that is the capacity not only to react but to respond personally to situations, taking risks and being prepared to make mistakes. It also helps to develop physical, emotional, and intellectual flexibility.

The development of language skills contributes to the development of the whole individual while traditional teaching concentrates more exclusively on linguistic objectives and, above all, on the acquisition of structure and lexis.

Bibliography

Adler, Mortimer Jerome & van Doren, Charles: *How to Read a Book*, New York, 1972, Simon and Schuster.

Appel, Joachim: *Diary of a Language Teacher*. 1995, Heinemann

Baker, Judith and Rinvolucri, Mario: *Unlocking Self-expression through NLP. 2005,* Delta Publishing, Surrey

Denjean, Jean: Die Praxis des Fremdsprachenunterrichts an der Waldorfschule, Stuttgart, 2000, Verlag Freies Geistesleben.

Dufeu, Bernard: *Wege zu einer Pädagogik des Seins.* Mainz, 2003, a szerző magánkiadása.

Hevesi Mihály: *A nyelvtanulás művészetéről.* Szeged, 2004, SzépNap könyvek.

Kiersch, Johannes: *Fremdsprachen in der Waldorfschule.* Stuttgart, 1992, Verlag Freies Geistesleben.

Lomb Kató: *Bábeli harmónia.* Budapest, 1983, Gondolat.

Lomb Kató: *Polyglot: How I learn languages.* California, 2008, Scott Alkire.

Knibbeler, Wil: The explorative-creative way, Tubingen, 1989, G. Narr Verlag.

Krashen, Stephen: *Second Language Acquisition and Second Language Learning,* California, 1981, Pergamon Press Inc.

Krashen, Stephen: *Second Language Acquisition and Second Language Learning*, 2002, University of Southern California, online version.

Krashen, Stephen: *The Power of Reading*, 2004, 2nd edition, Heinemann.

Lutzker, Peter: *The Art of Foreign Language Teaching*, Tübingen, 2007, Franke Verlag,

Matthews, Paul: *Sing Me the Creation,* 1996, Hawthorn Press.

Pinker, Steven: *A nyelvi ösztön*. Budapest, 1999, Typotex.

Russell, Charles William: *The Life of Cardinal Mezzofanti*. London, 1858, Longman, Brown, and Co.

Rinvolucri, Mario: *Humanising Your Coursebook: Activities to Bring Your Classroom to Life,* Surrey, 2002, Delta Publishing.

Rinvolucri, Mario: *Grammar Games – Cognitive, affective and drama activities for EFL,* 1994, Cambridge University Press.

Schiffler, Ludger: *Learning by doing im Fremdsprachenunterricht – Handlungsund partnerorientierter Fremdsprachenunterricht mit und ohne Lehrbuch*, 2004, Freie Universitaet Berlin – online.

Schiffler, Ludger: *Fremdsprachen effektiver lehren und lernen – Beide Gehirnhälften aktivieren*. Berlin, 2002, (Hrsg.) Auer.

Schliemann, Heinrich: *Abenteuer meines Lebens.* 1990, Brockhaus,

Templeton, Alec: *Teaching English to Teens and Preteens.* Szeged, 2007, SzépNap könyvek.

Ur, Penny: A Course in Language Teaching. Practice and Theory. Cambridge, 1991.

Ur, Penny: *Discussions That Work*, 1994, Cambridge

Ur, Penny and Wright, Andrew: *Five-Minute Activities: A Resource Book of Short Activities.* 1992, Cambridge University Press

www.ingramcontent.com/pod-product-compliance
Lightning Source LLC
Chambersburg PA
CBHW061318120726
48001CB00002B/579